# FLOWERS OF WONDER

A Coloring Book of
Fabulous Fantasy Flowers

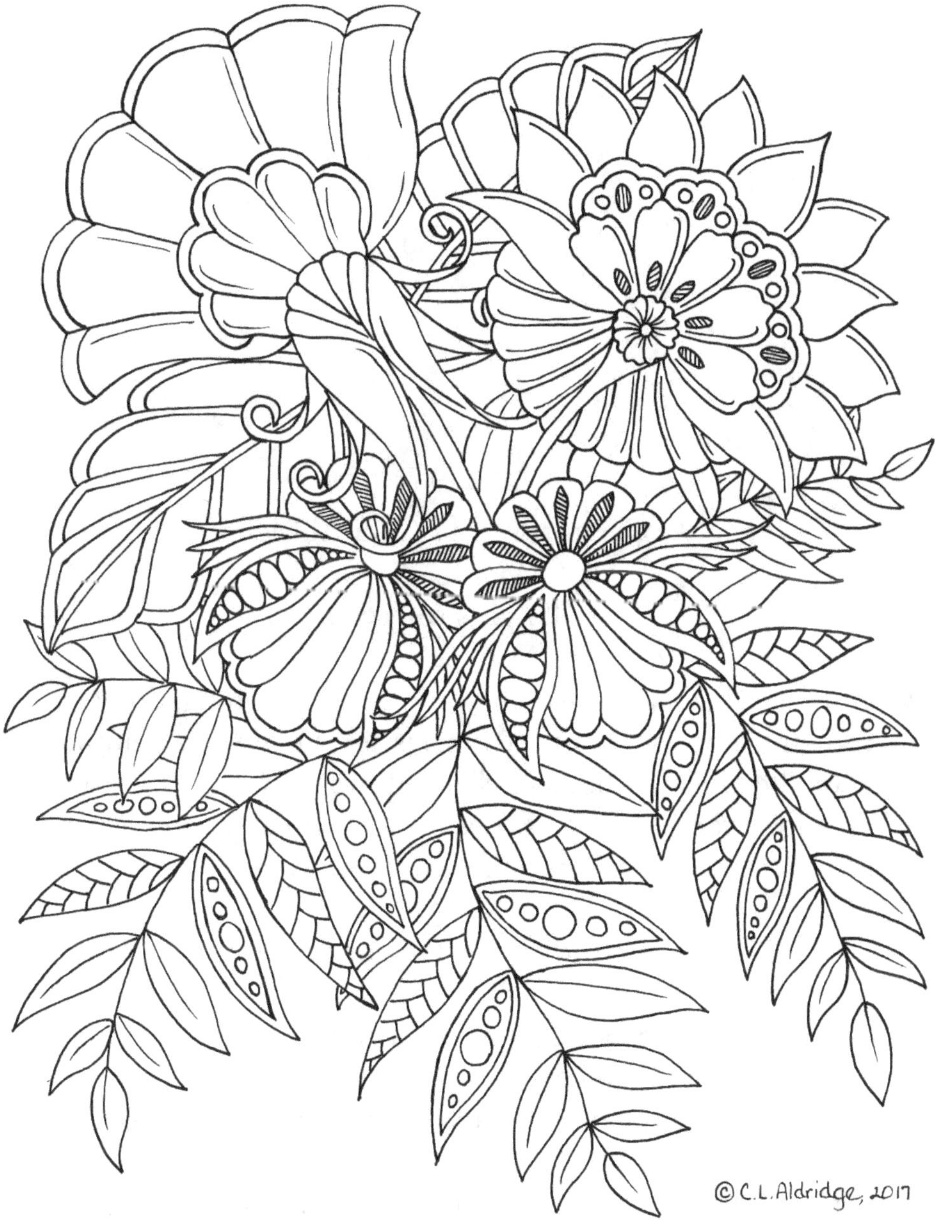

Illustrations by: C. L. Aldridge

Copyright © 2017 C. L. Aldridge

All rights reserved.

In accordance with the U.S. Copyright Act of 1976, the scanning, uploading, and electronic sharing of any part of this book without the permission of the artist/author constitutes unlawful piracy and theft of the artist/author's intellectual property. If you would like to use material from the book (other than for review purposes), prior written permission must be obtained by contacting the artist/author at:

CLAldridgeArt@gmail.com

Or visit me on Facebook at: www.facebook.com/CLAldridgeArt
Or visit my website at: www.CLAldridgeArt.com
Or follow me on Twitter and Instagram: @CLAldridgeArt

Thank You for your support of the artist/author's rights.

ISBN-13:978-1975872984
ISBN-10:1975872983

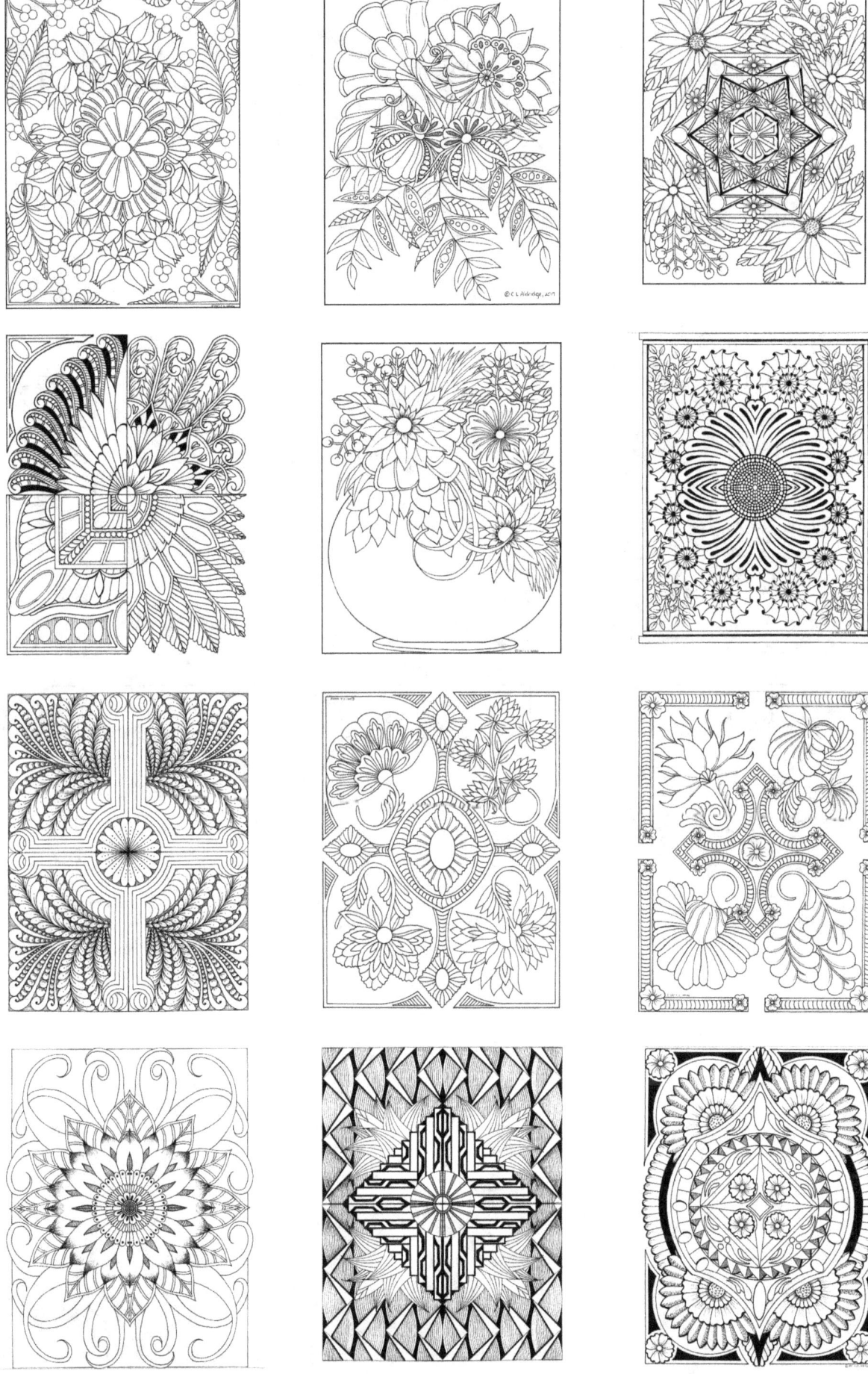

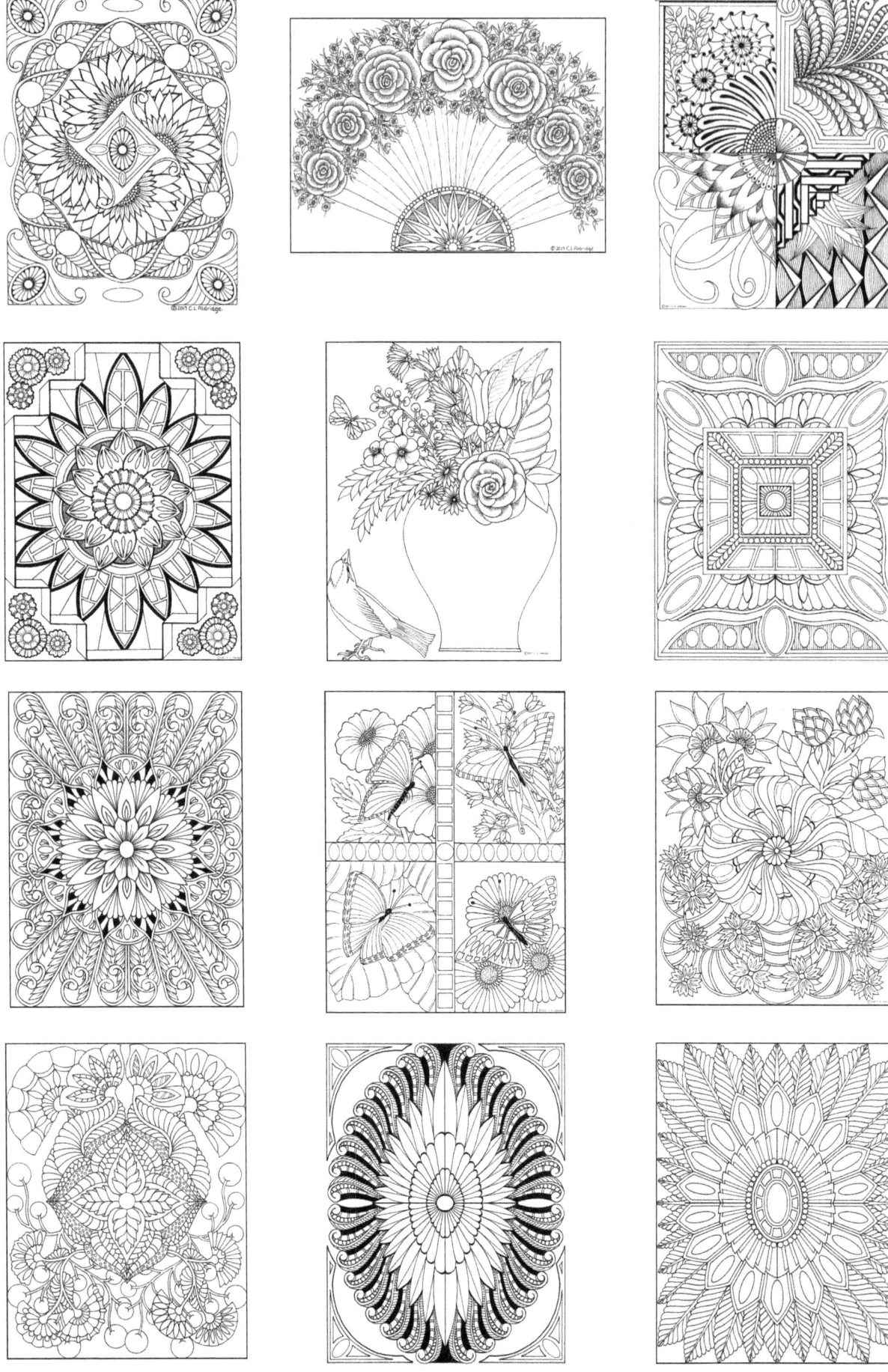

# PLUS A FULL SET OF 24 - CRAFT/GREETING CARD SIZE,
Printed 2 per page— sample layouts below

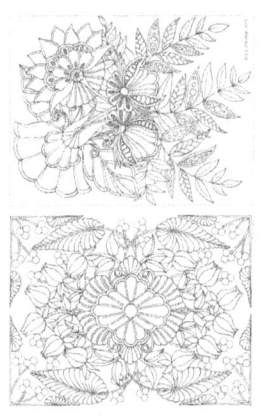
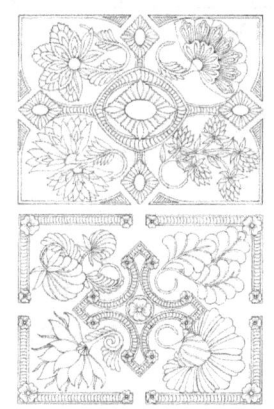
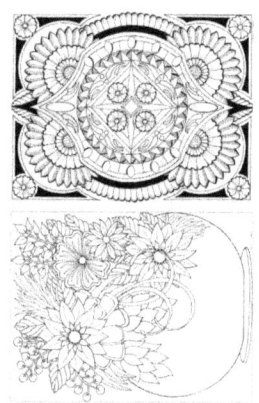

# PLUS 6 BONUS PAGES!

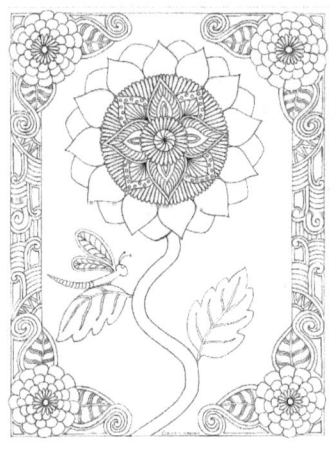
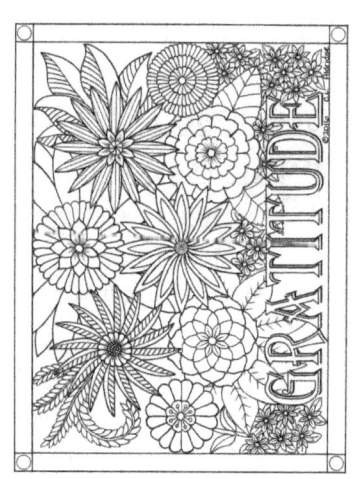
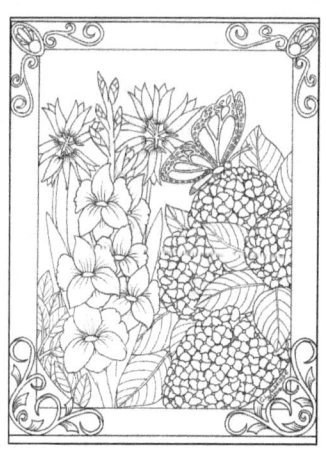
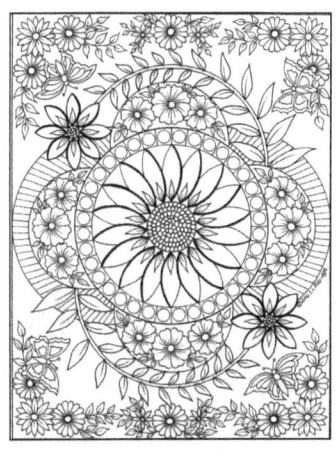
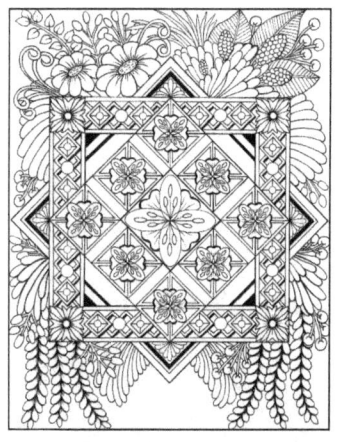
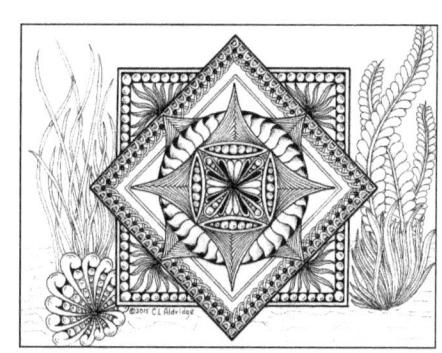

# Also by C. L. Aldridge

## Flowers and Dreams
A Coloring Book of Beautiful Botanical Symmetry

- This book is so elegant that when you finish coloring it you want to frame every one! - Jun. 16, 2016 ~ *Amazon Customer* (now in it's 2nd Edition), first pub. Jan. 7, 2016

## Adult Coloring Book of Flower Inspirations
Beautiful Floral Patterns, Botanical Mandalas,
Gemstones, Lovely Words and More!

- C. L. Aldridge has hit it out of the ballpark again! - June 10, 2016 ~ *E. Siegel* (pub. April 24, 2016)

## Flowers and Flyers
Adult Coloring Book of Flowers, Songbirds, Hummingbirds,
Butterflies, Owls, Ornamentals and More!

- I have all 3 of C L Aldridge's books. These 3 are at the top of my list! - Sept. 30, 2016 ~ *C. Ames* (published Aug. 24, 2016)

## Travel Size Book of Flowers, Birds Butterflies and More!
Your Coloring Book for the Road.

- Measures 6" x 9", just the right size to tuck in a purse, a travel bag or a desk drawer.

## Flowers and Whimsy
Adult Coloring Book of
Fun to Color Ornamental Floral Patterns,
Whimsical Butterflies, Dragonflies and More!

- Drop dead gorgeous drawings, one after another. Every page is a feast for the eyes. All of her books are glorious. –April 28, 2017 ~ *J. Fanning* (published Dec. 3, 2016)

## Flowers of Fantasy
A Coloring Book of Fantastical Floral Designs

- C.L. Aldridge has outdone herself!!! Beautiful and fun images to color!!! - July 18, 2017 ~ WitchyKat (Pub. June 3, 2017)

This book is dedicated to the fans at:
C. L. Aldridge's, Coloring in Bloom-Coloring Club
on Facebook, whose faith in my Art, and whose daily encouragement,
brings such joy to my life. Also to my dear friend and fellow artist
Susan Curry, for her enthusiasm and support!

A very special thank you to colorists: Virginia Sanders Cole,
Susan Curry, and Elizabeth Zack Siegel for so generously
allowing me to use their colored renderings of my drawings
on the cover of this book.

\* \* \* \* \*

## IMPORTANT INFORMATION FOR USING THIS BOOK

- This book contains 48 hand-drawn illustrations to color, each is printed SINGLE SIDED (back is blank). Plus 6 additional bonus pages!

- Illustrations are printed in TWO SIZES, a full size page and a crafters size (suitable for a 5" x 7" frame, mounting to a greeting card face or scrapbook page, etc). Please note the crafters sizes are also single sided and are printed two on a page.

- The pages are printed on #60 lb bright white paper which performs well for all brands of colored pencils and crayons, without the need of a blotter page.

- To avoid any "Uh Oh's" and the associated disappointment, **Marker and Gel Pen users are STRONGLY ENCOURAGED to USE A BLOTTER SHEET** behind the drawing to avoid any possibility of bleed through to the next page. Several blank blotter and color testing pages are provided at the end of this book.

- Most IMPORTANT of all: Relax, have fun, stand-up and stretch often, and remember that sometimes the most beautiful things come from what we think at first are mistakes, but which turn out to be art's way of working magic!

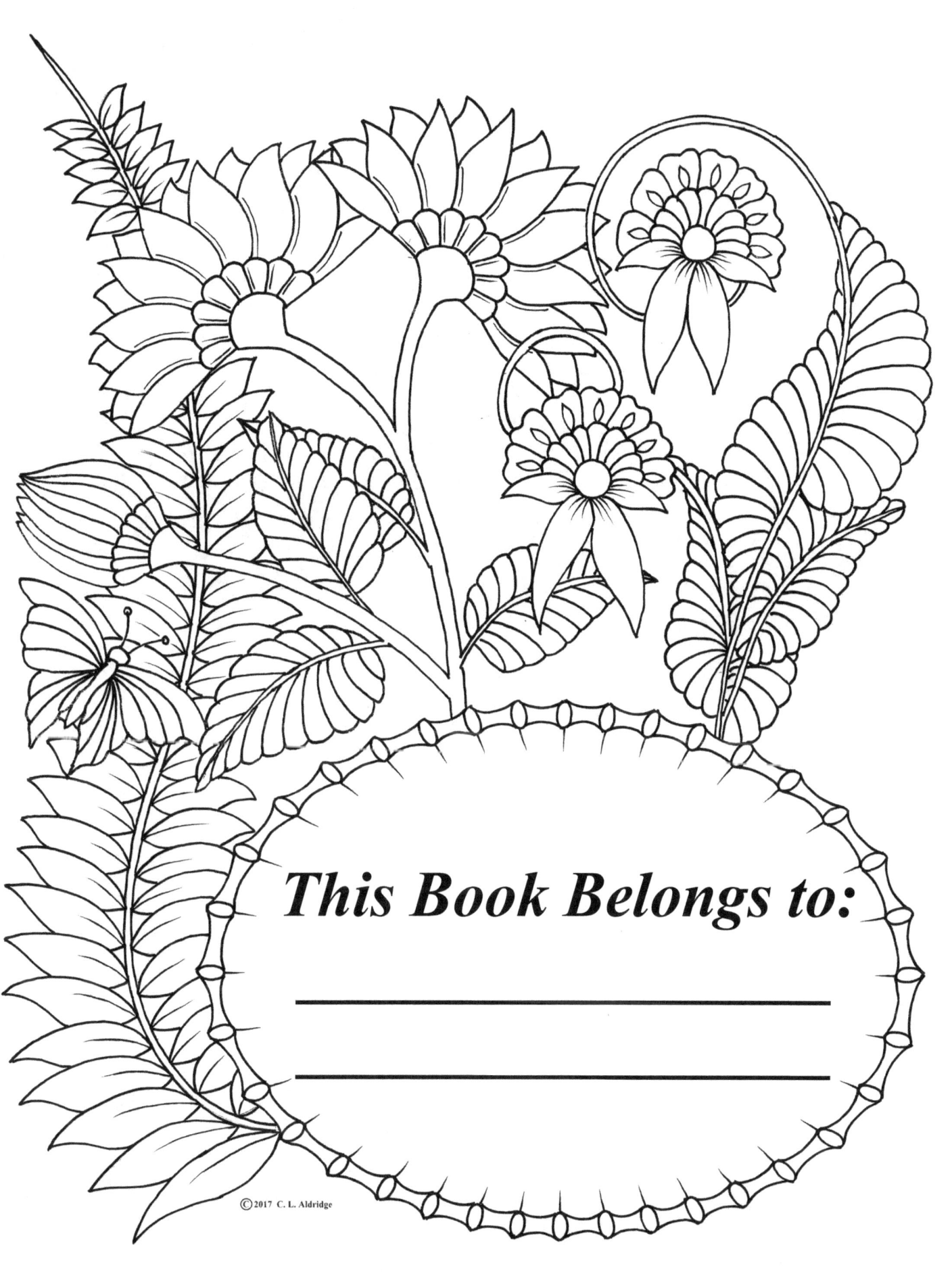

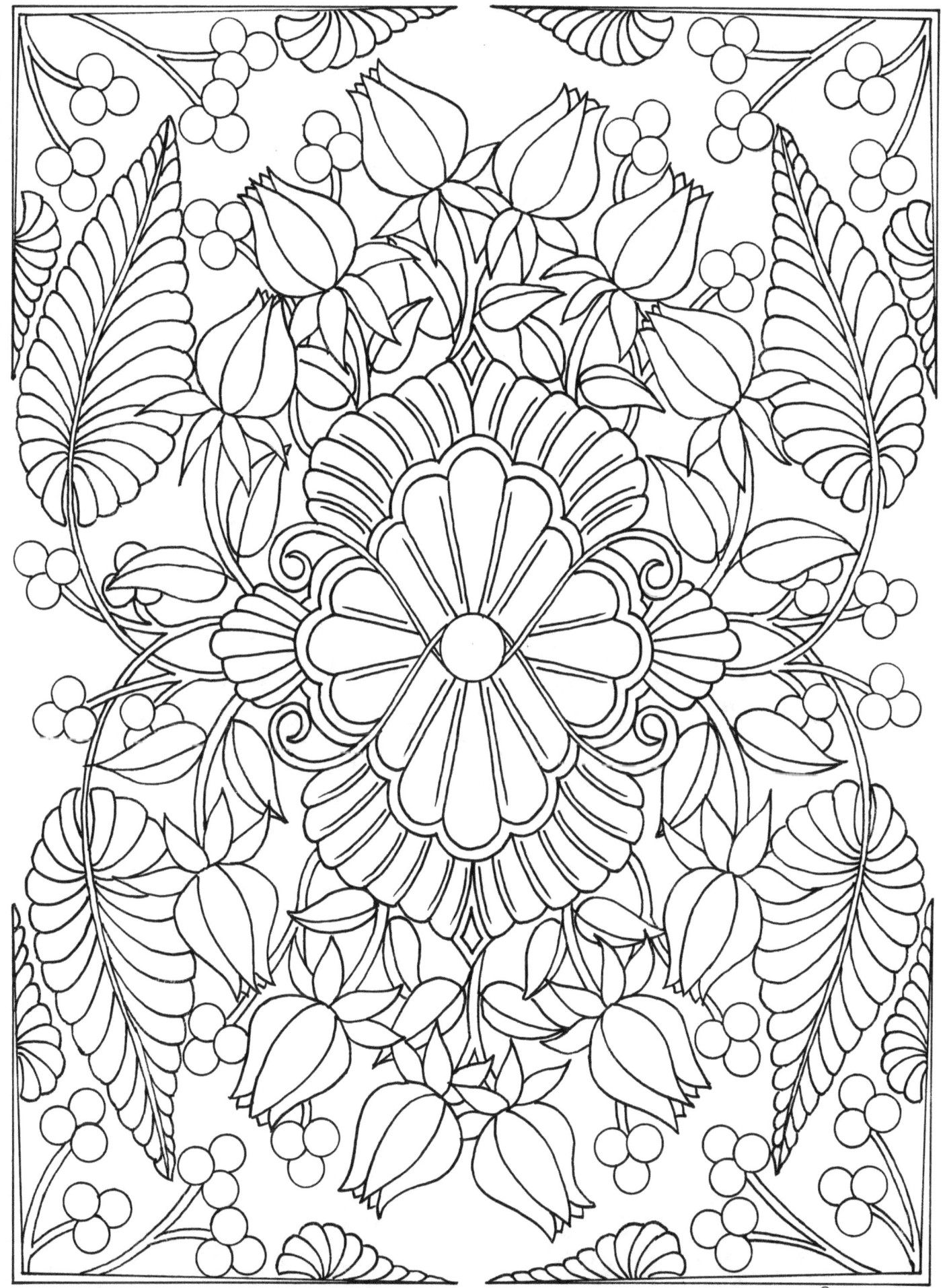

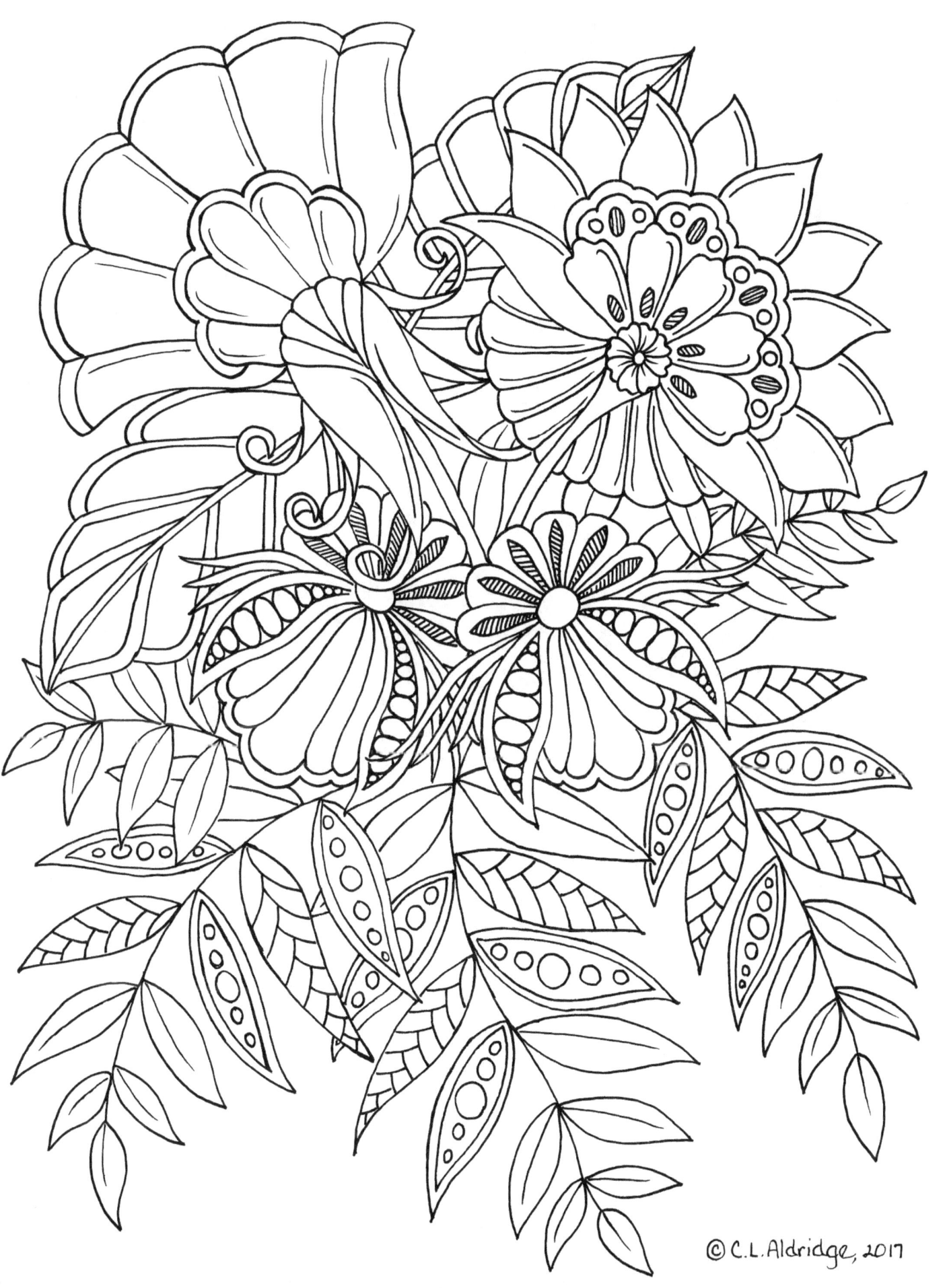

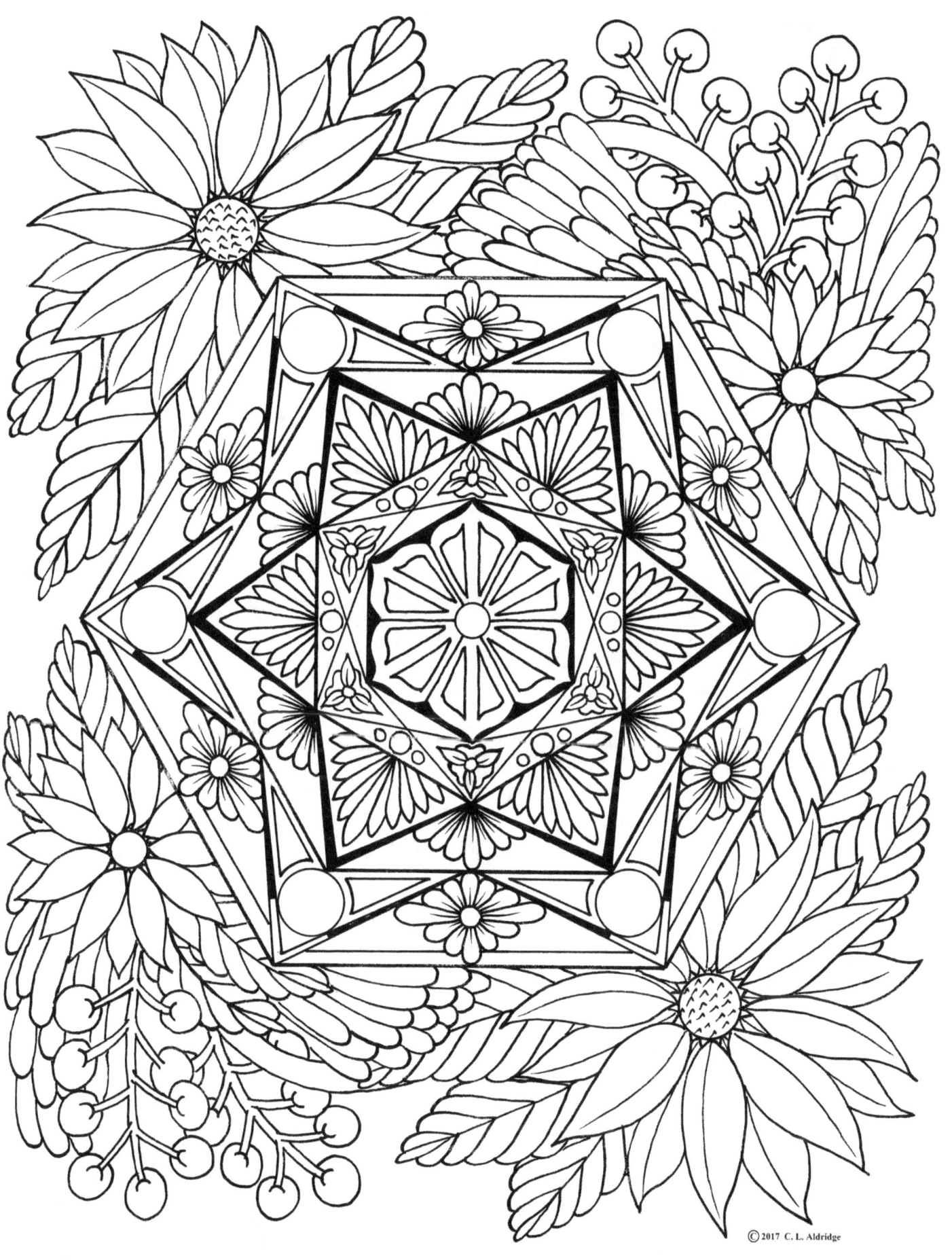

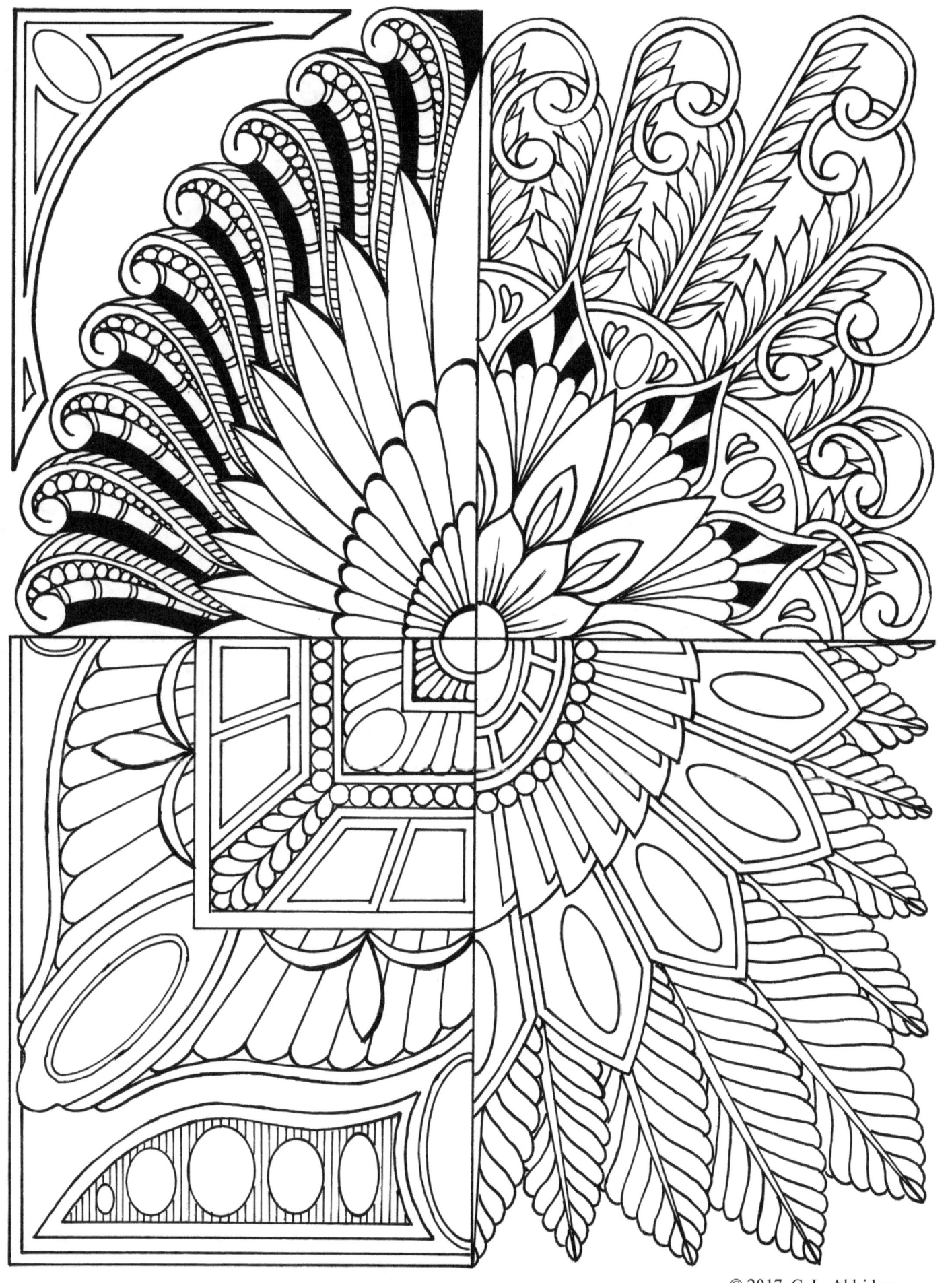

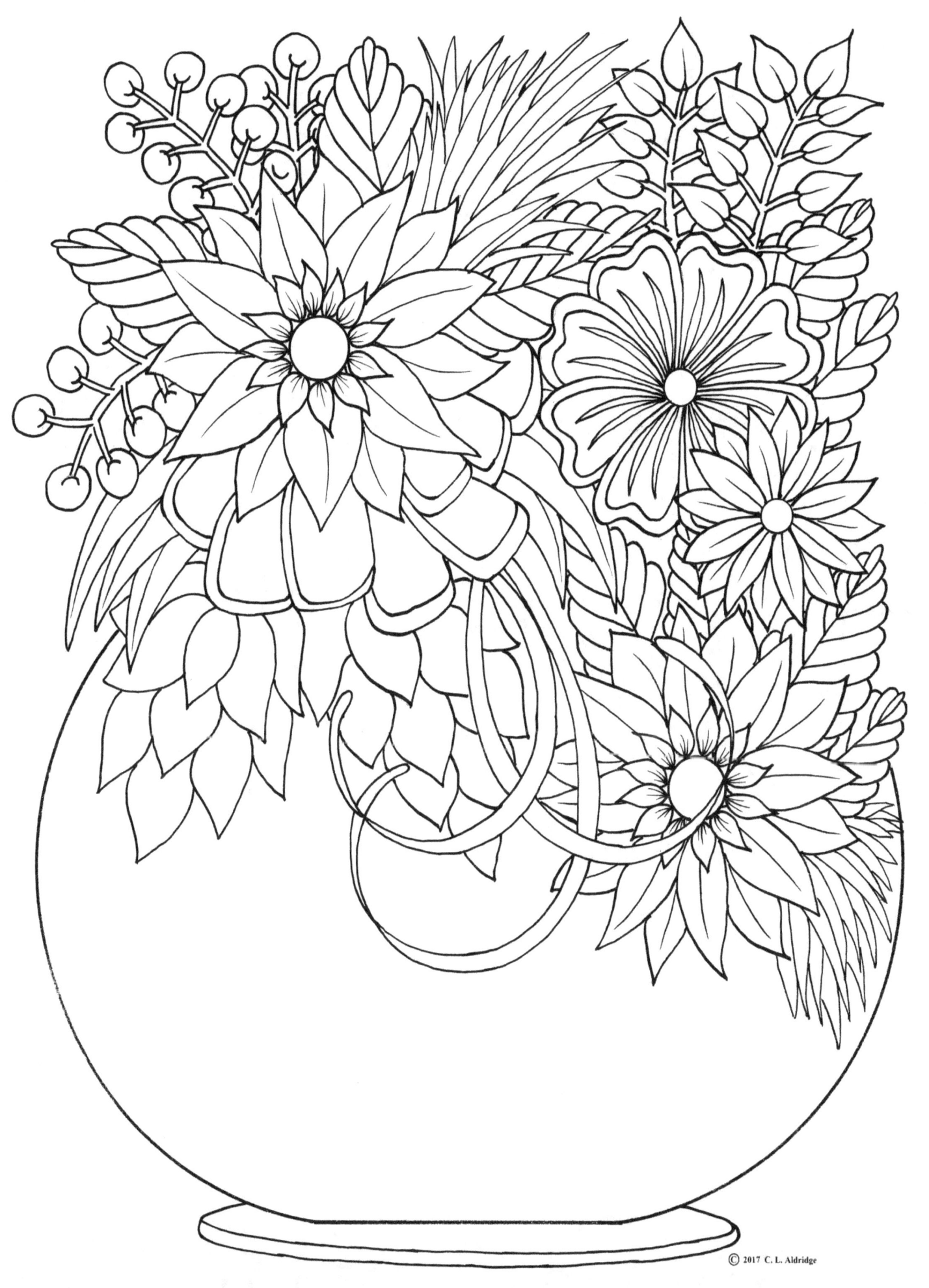

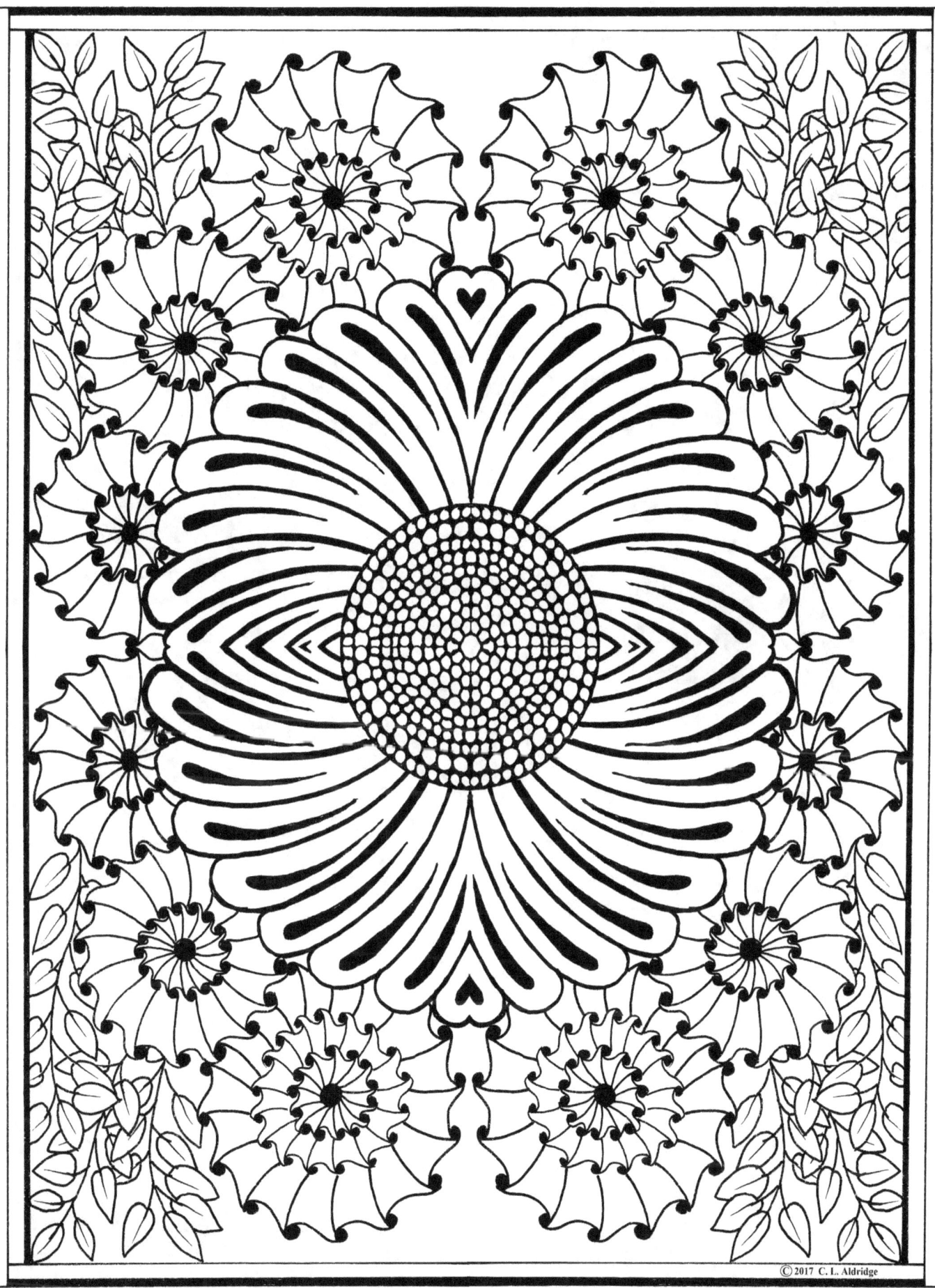

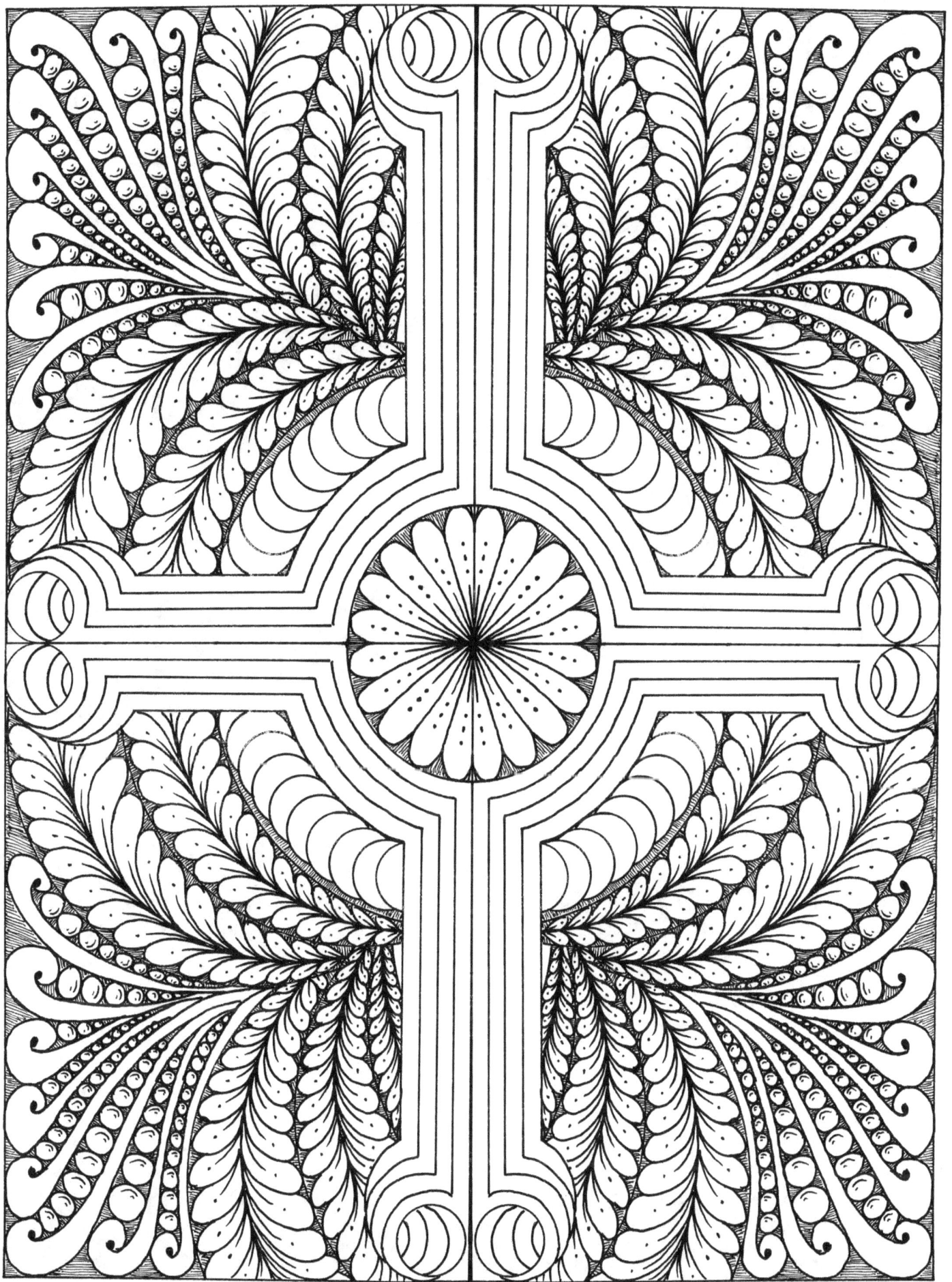

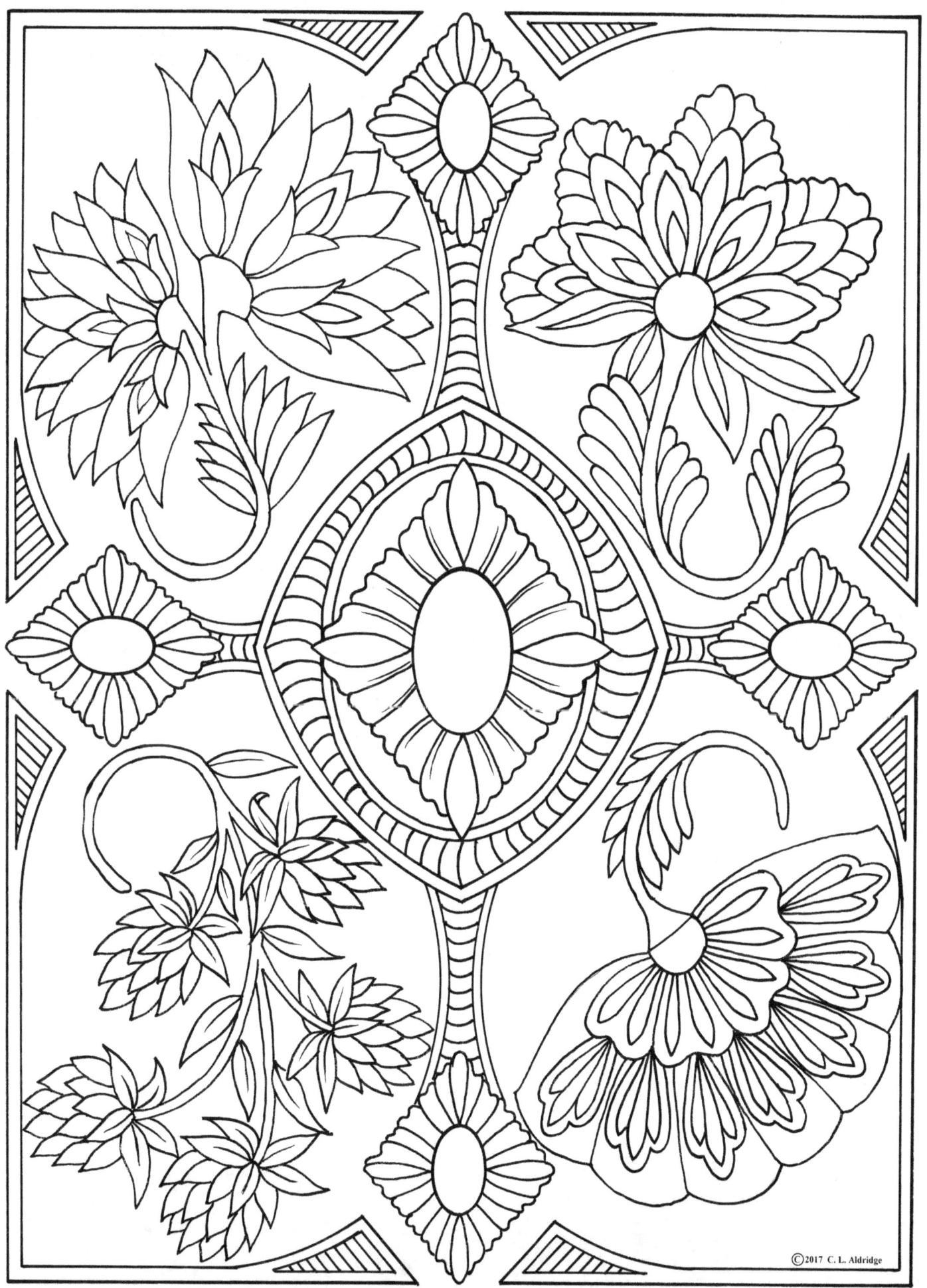

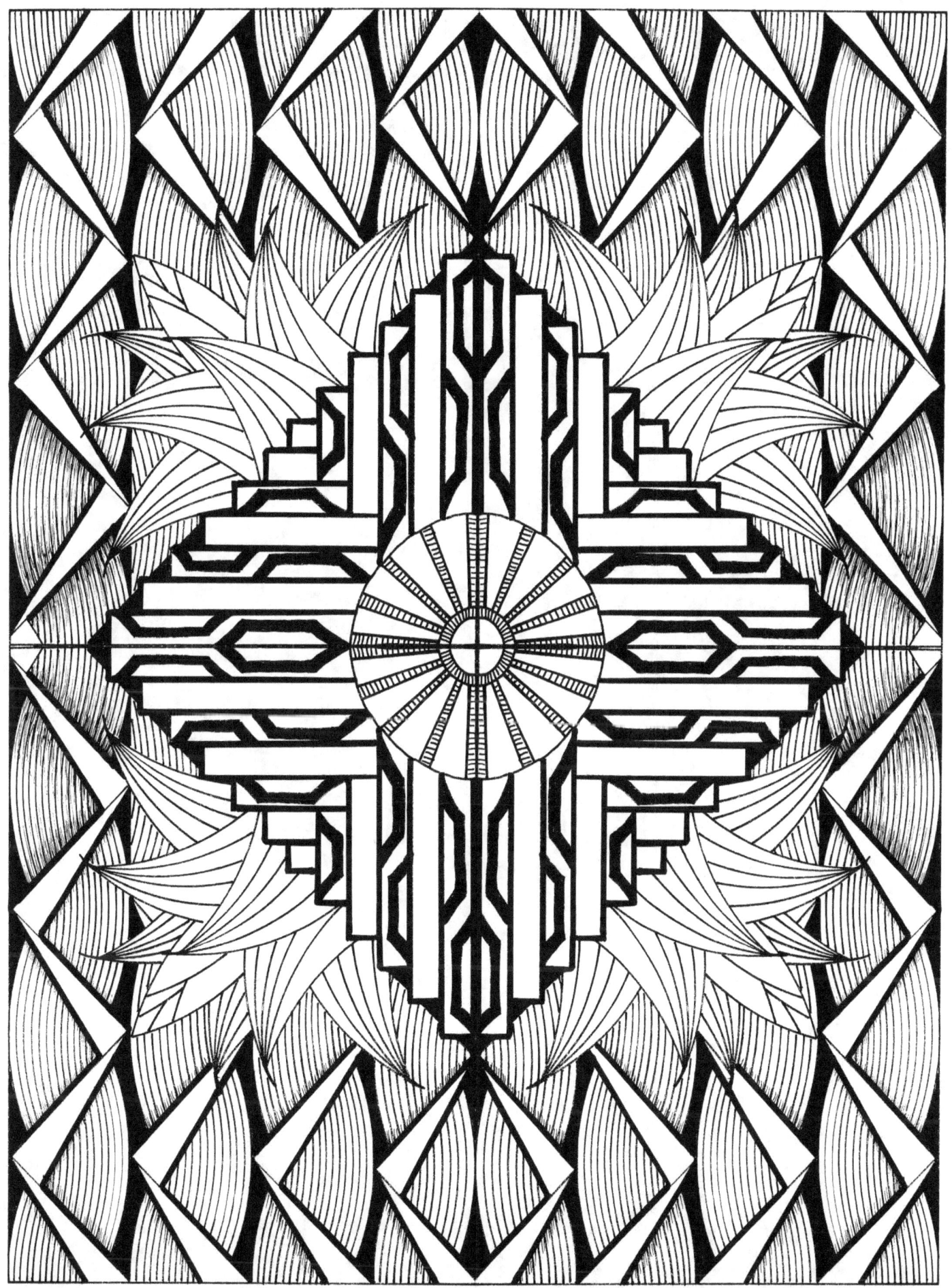

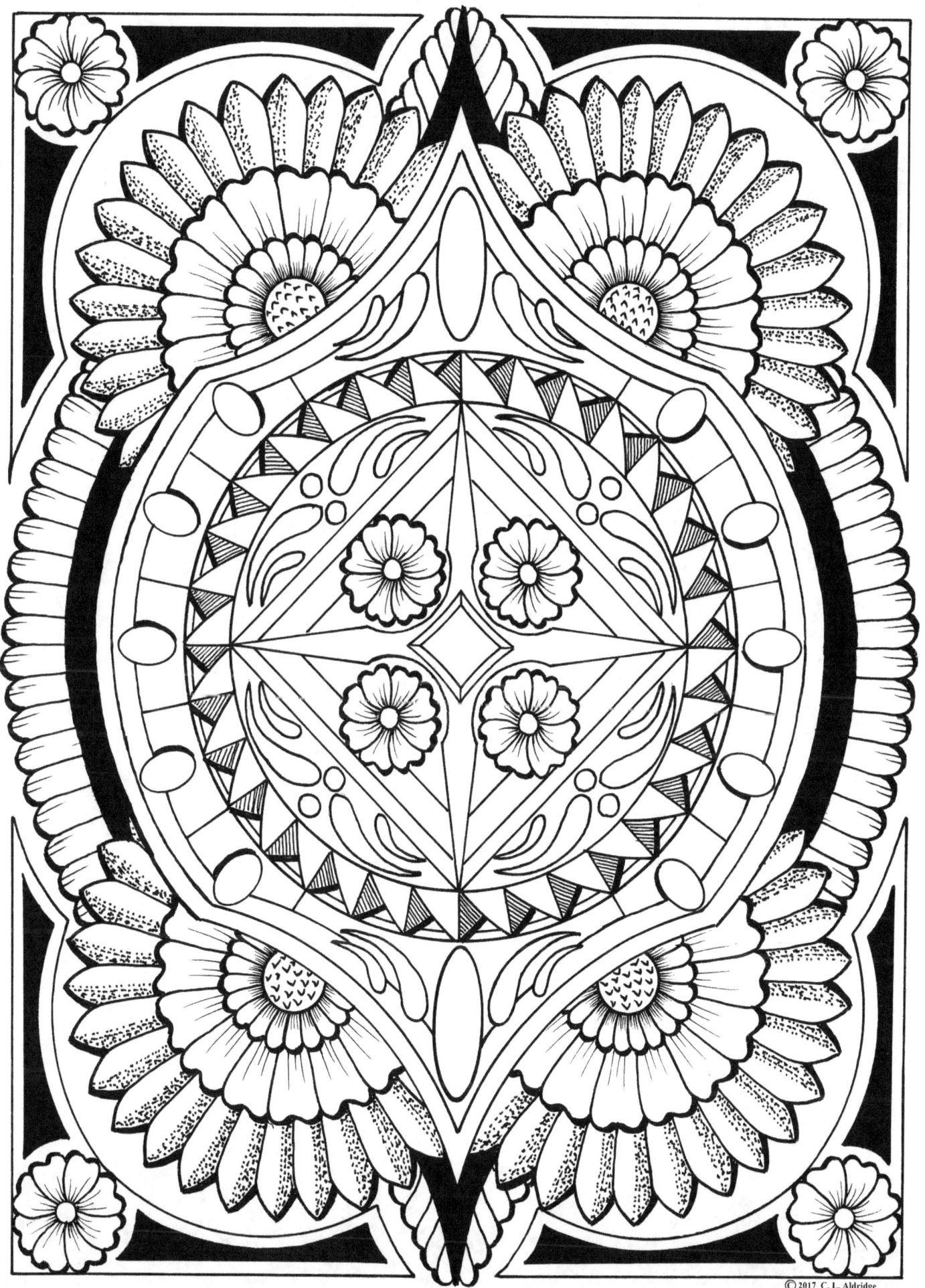

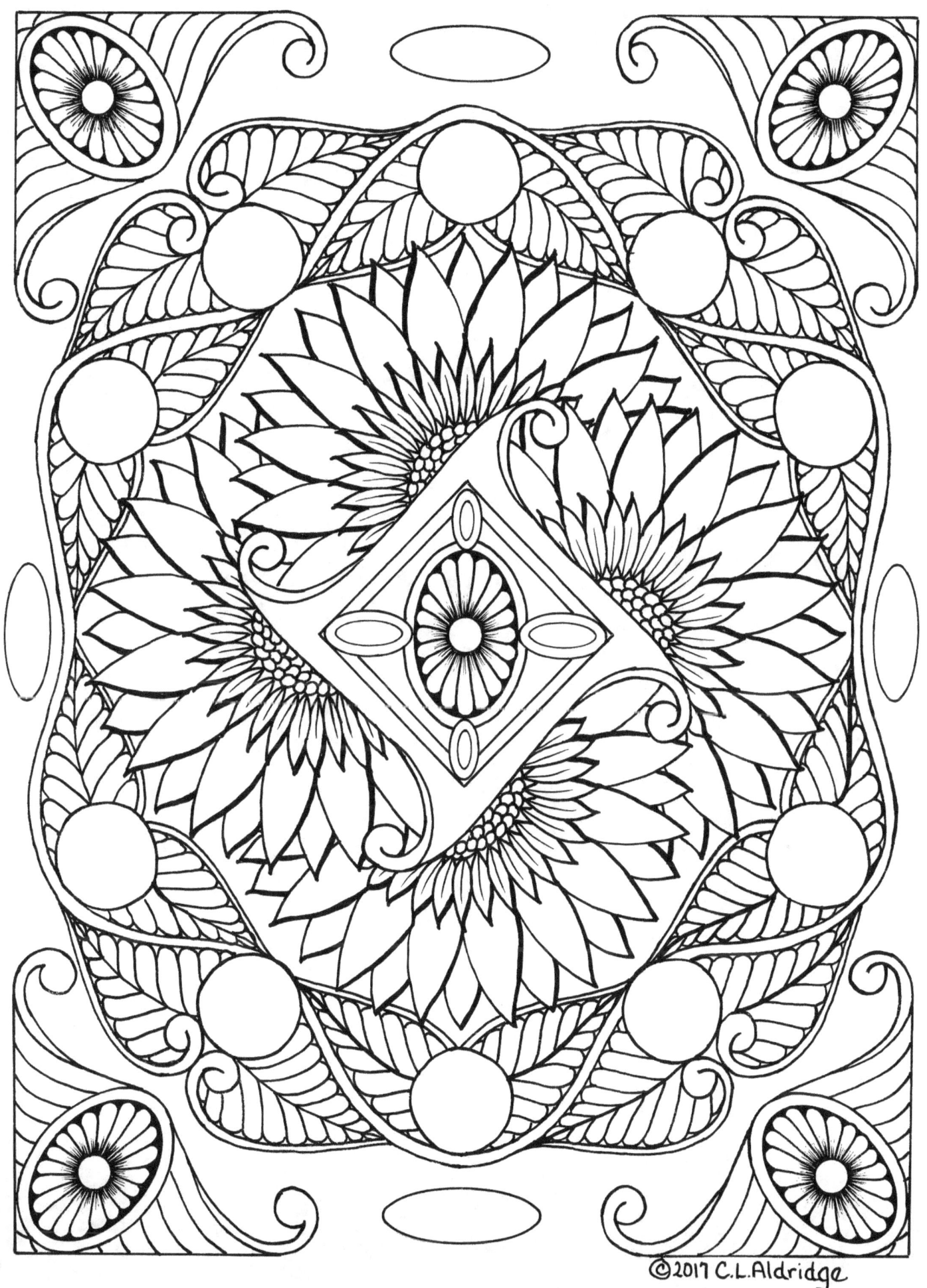

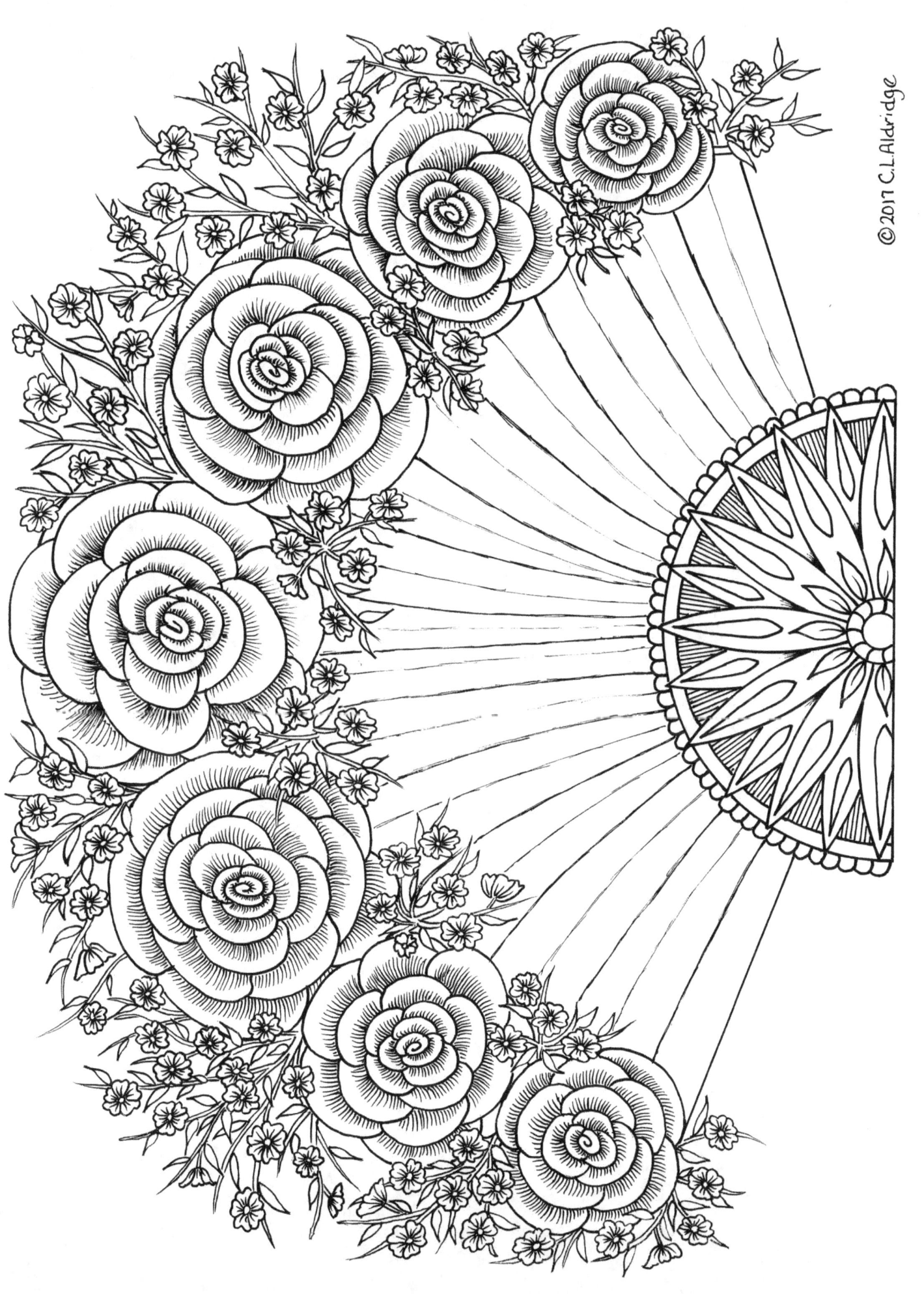

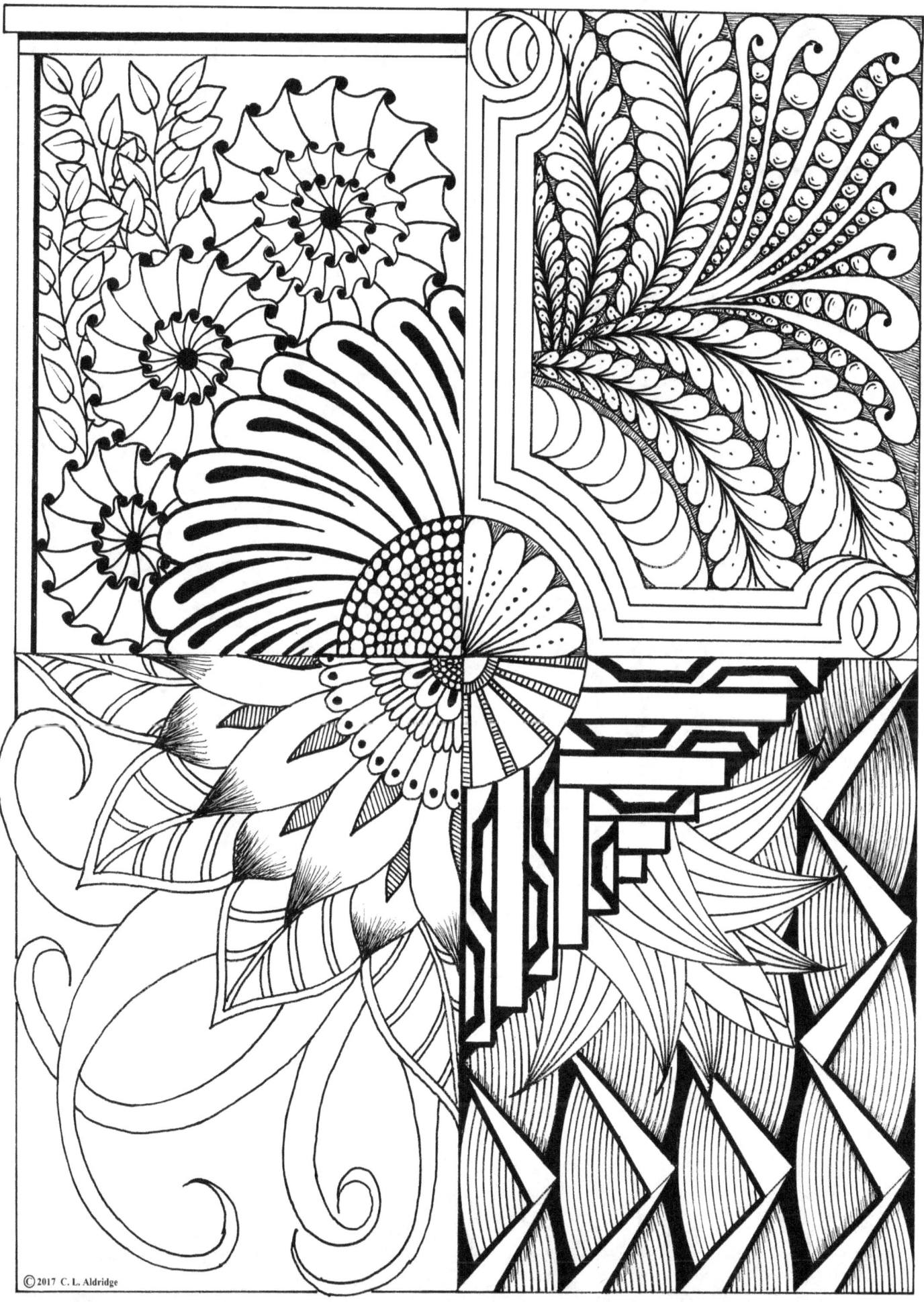

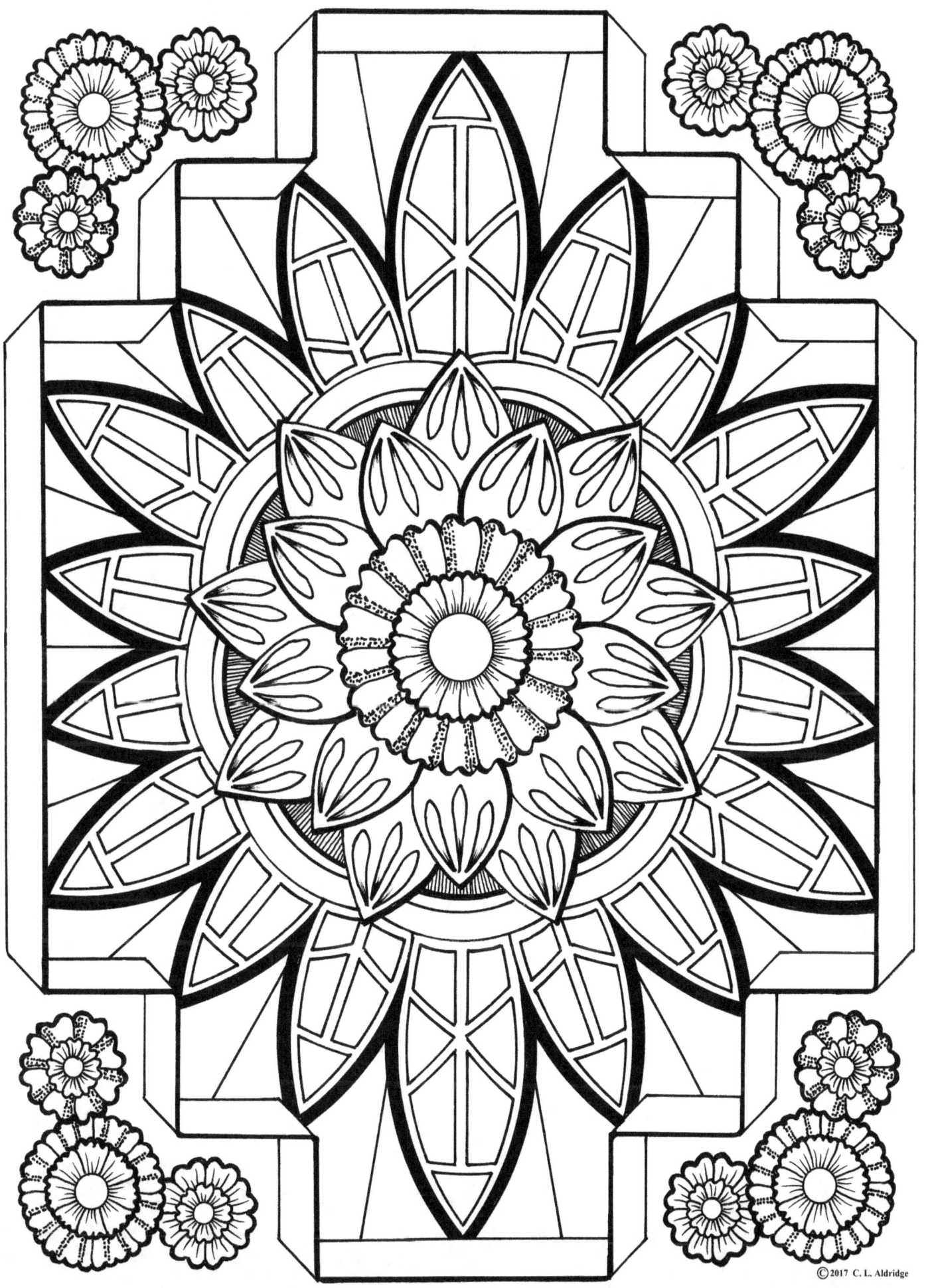

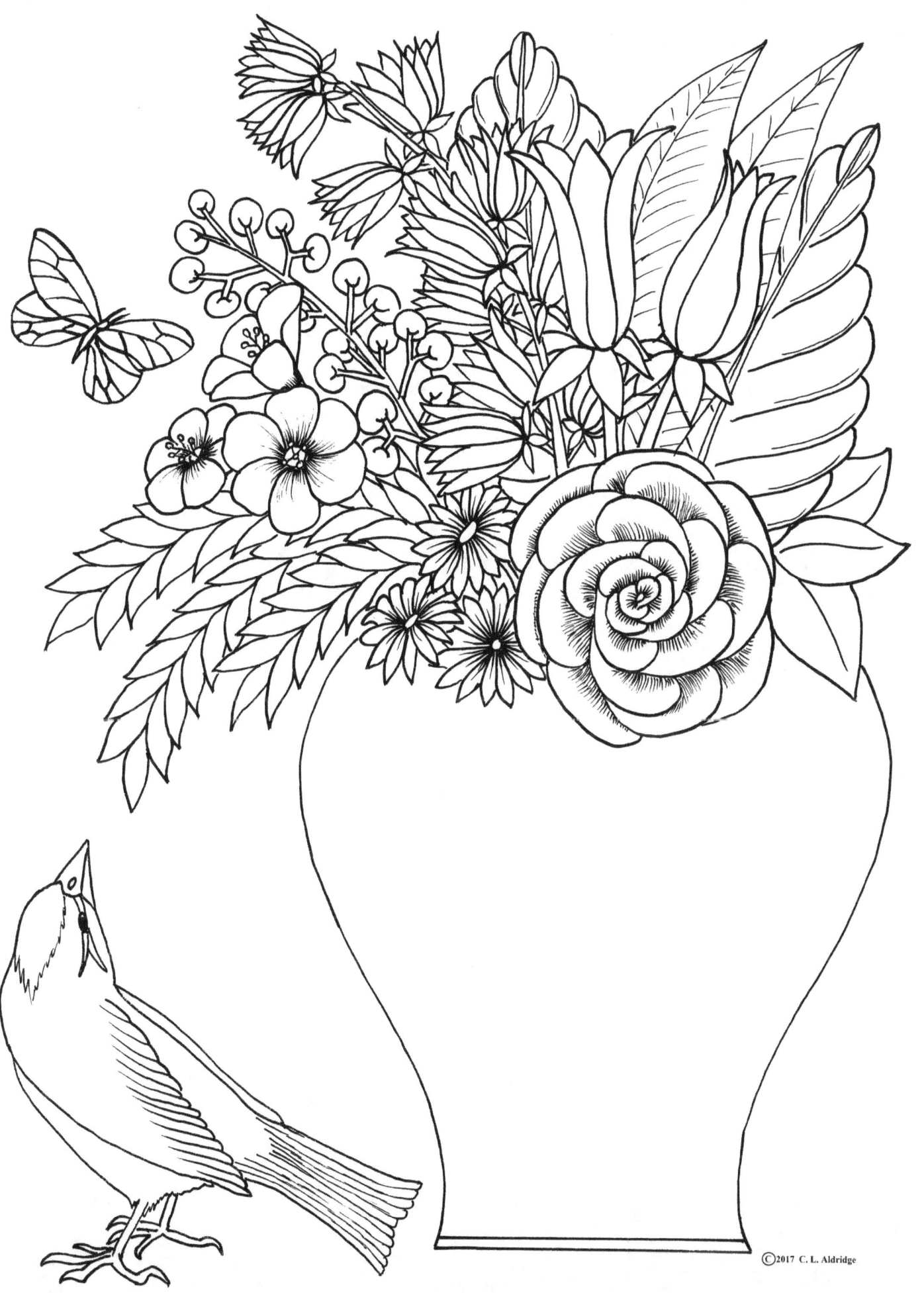

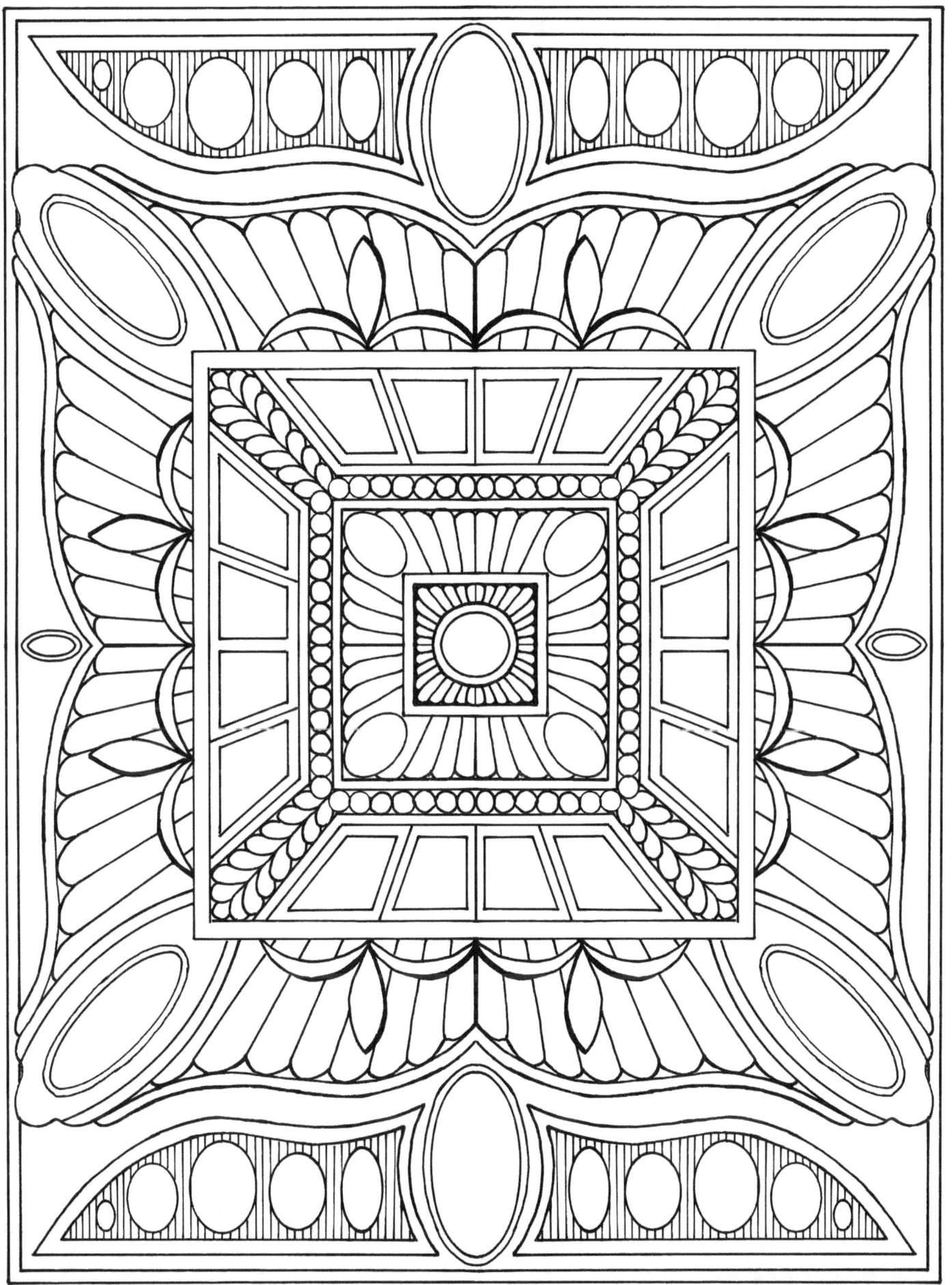

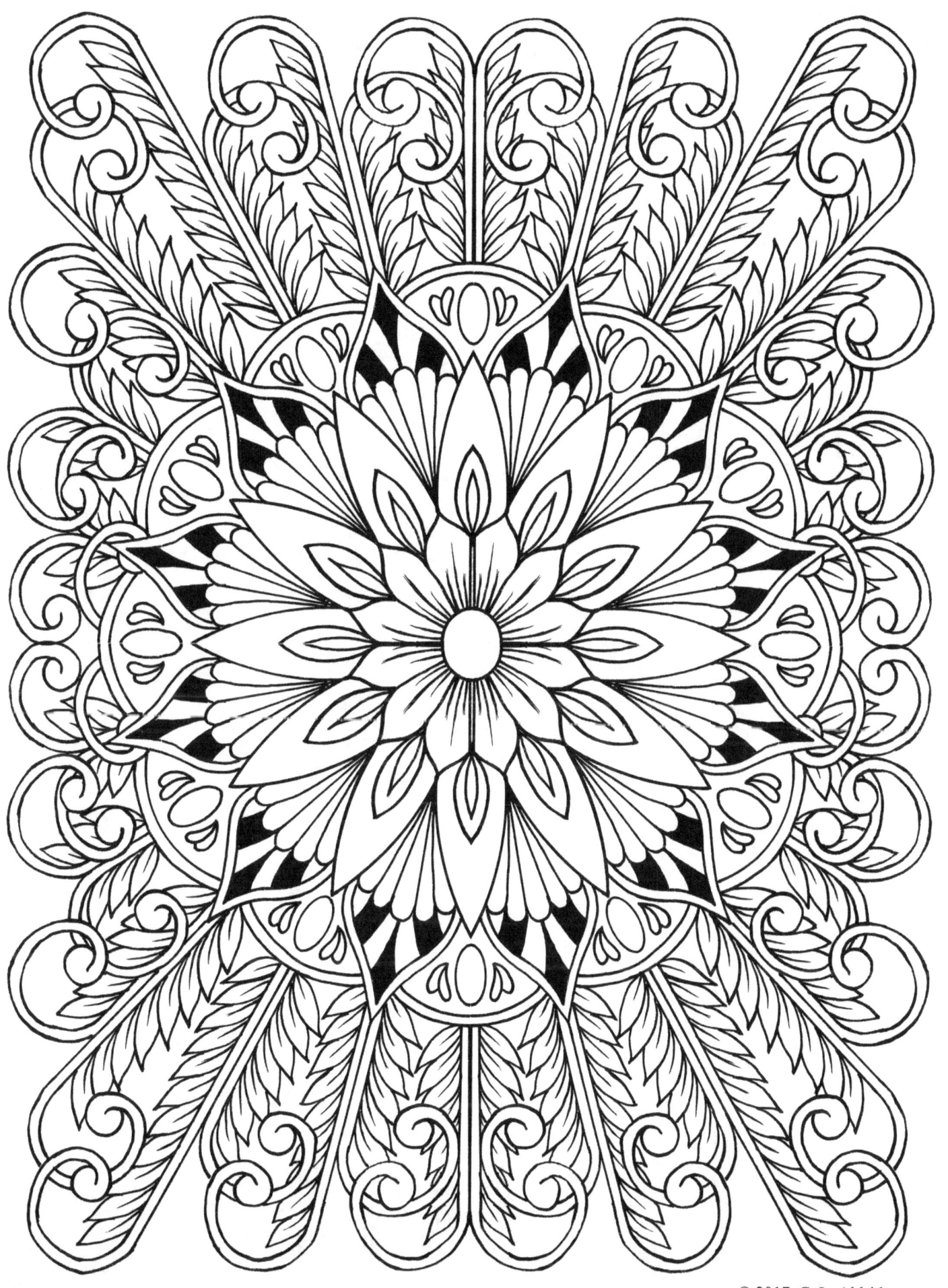

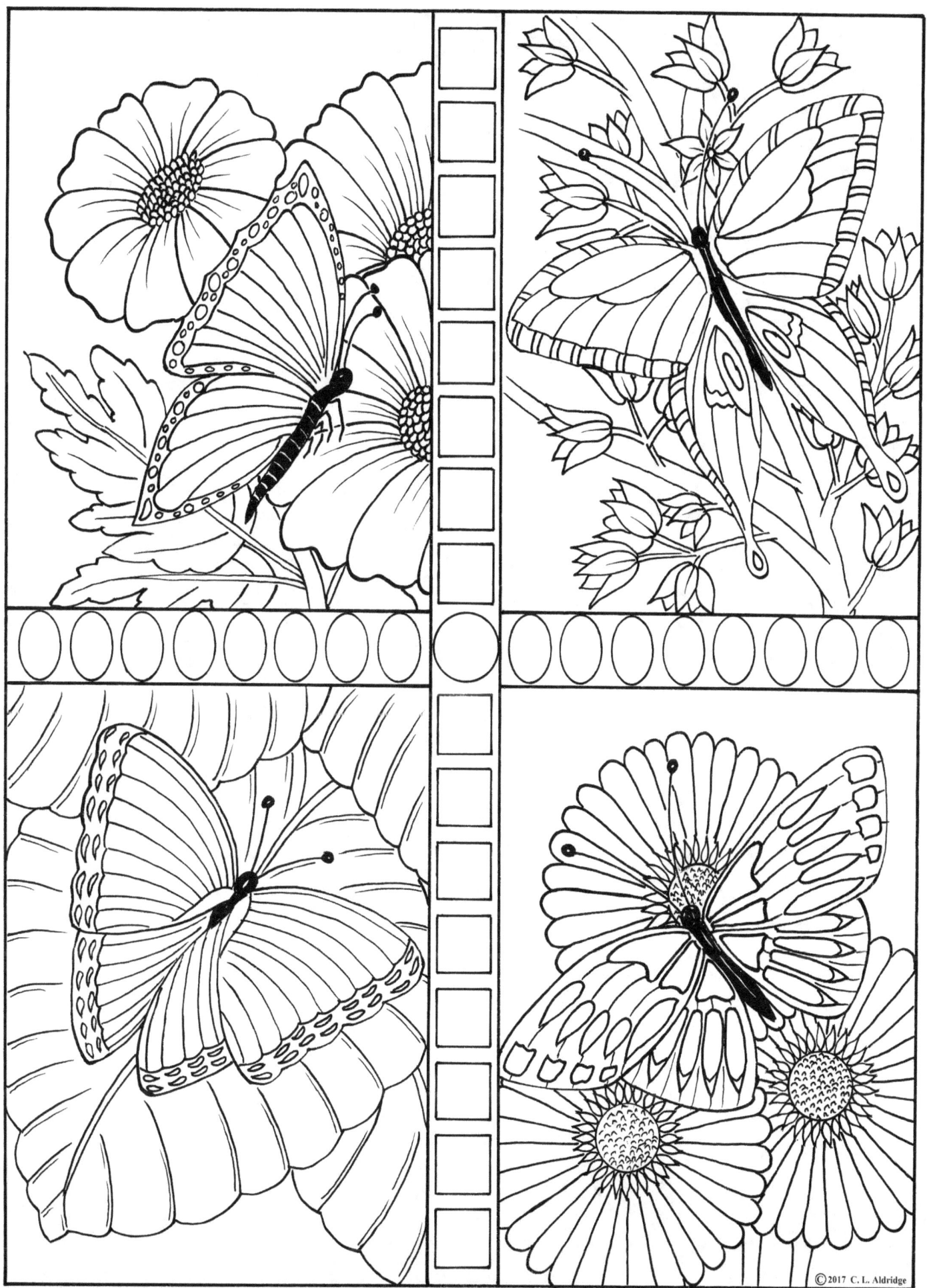

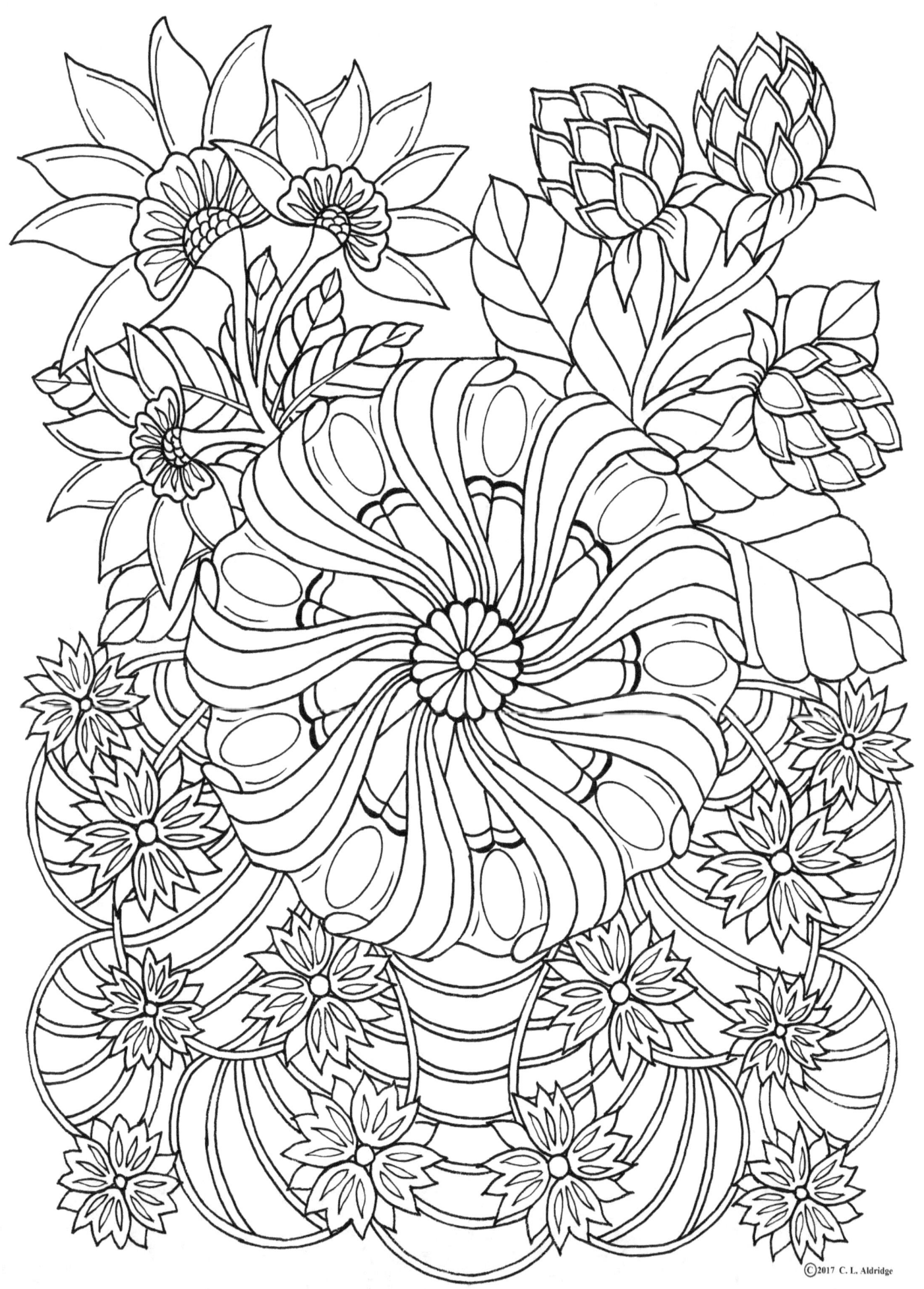

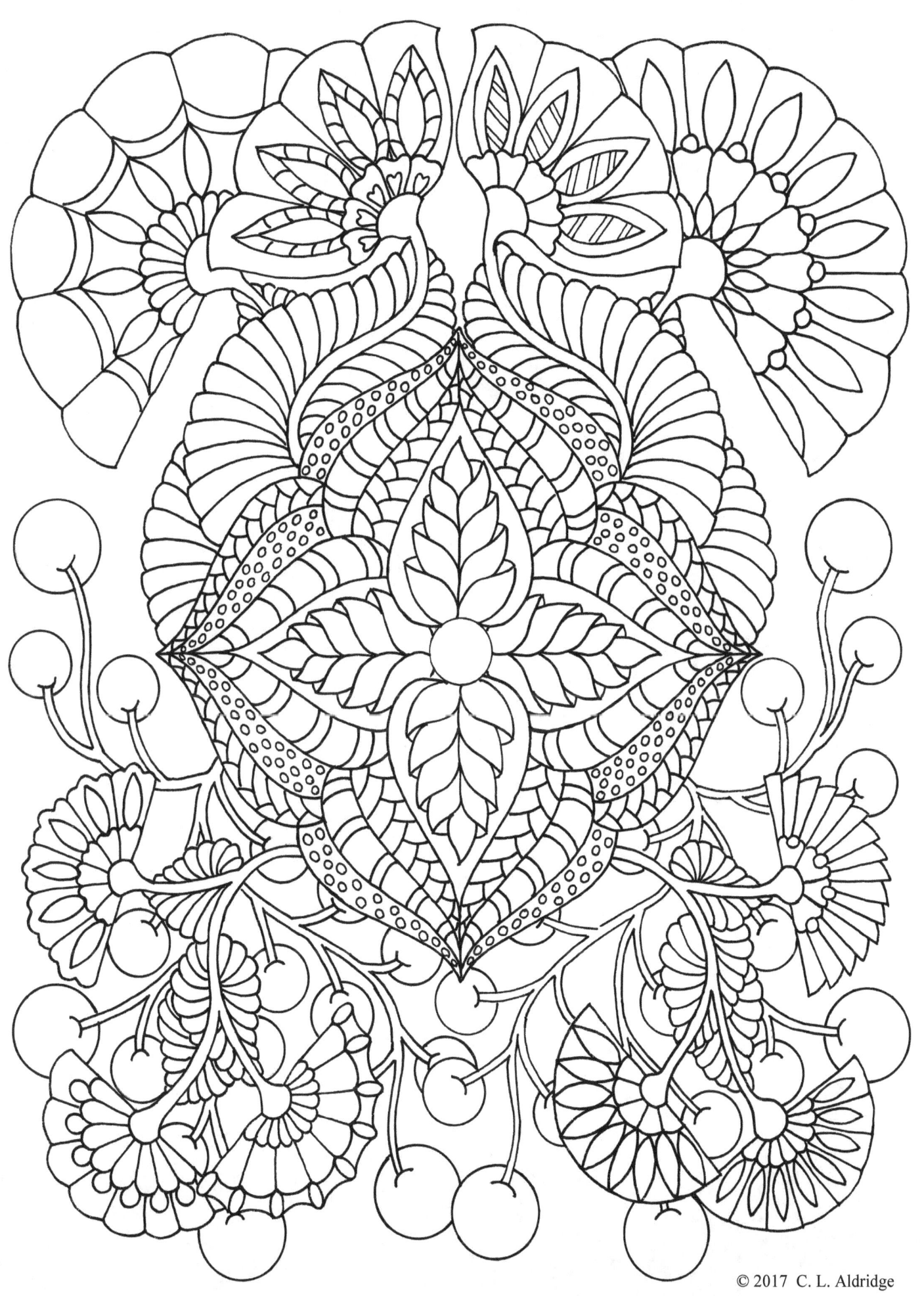

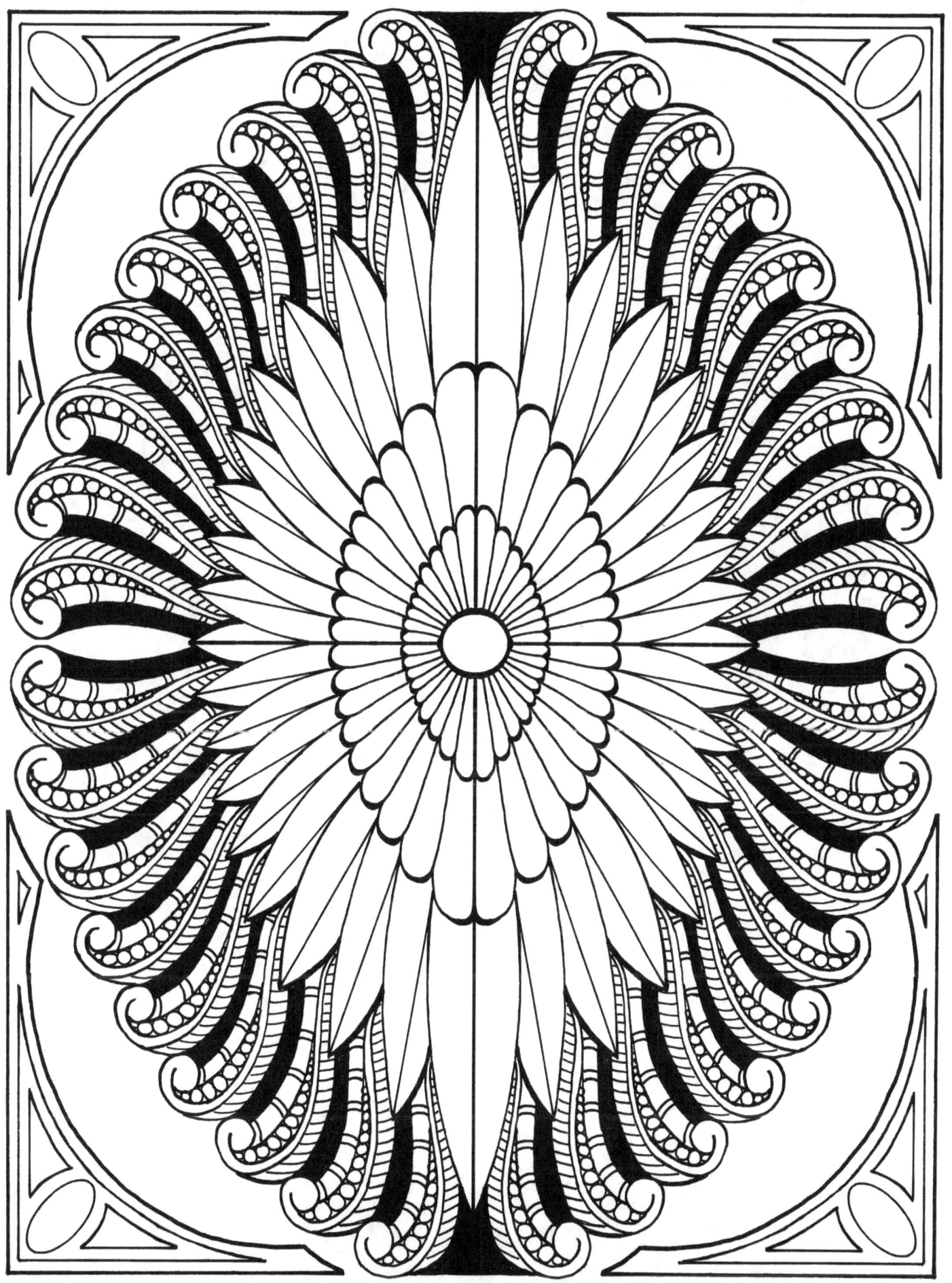

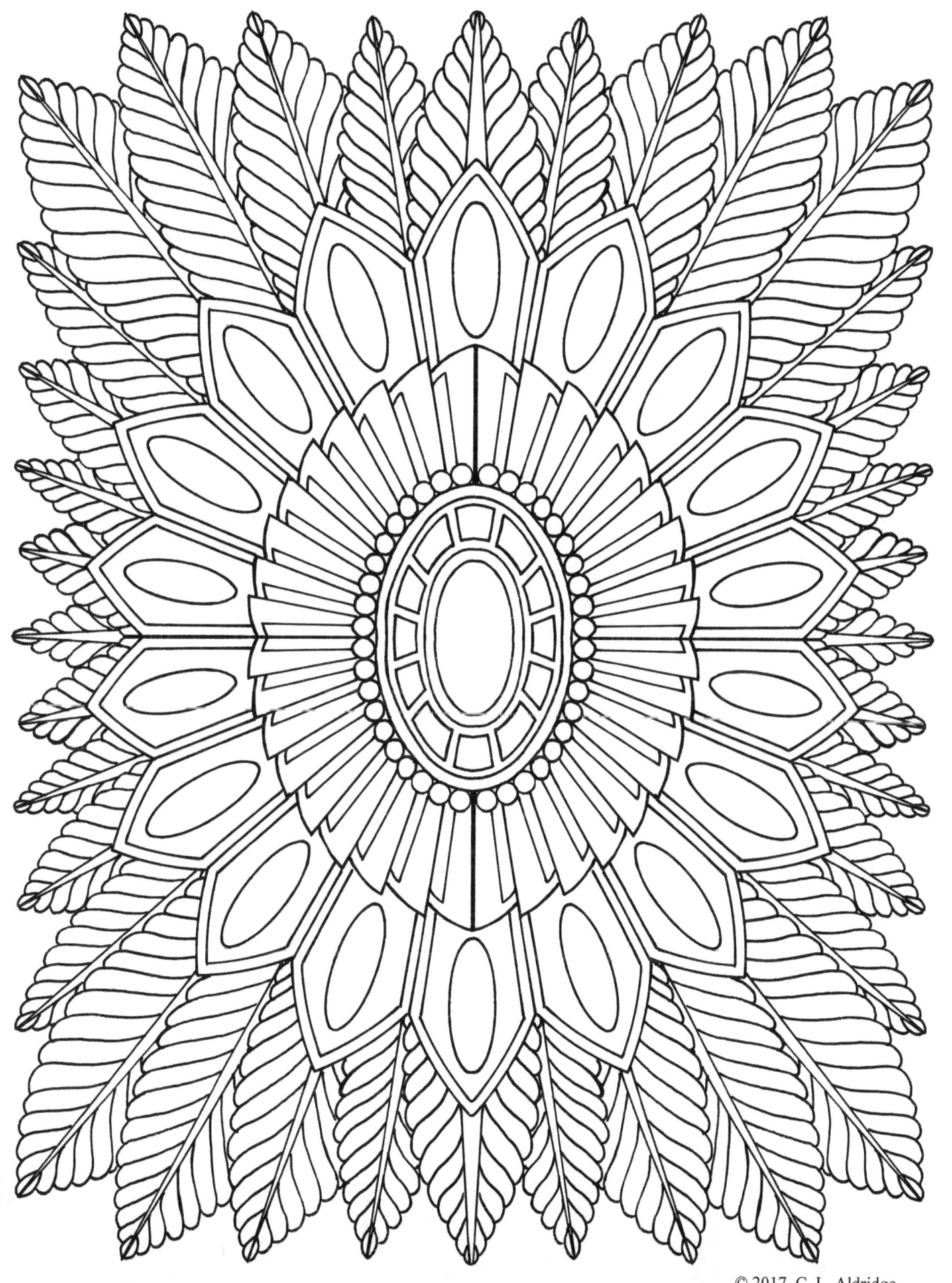

# A FULL SET OF CRAFT/GREETING CARD BONUS PAGES

Adapted versions of the larger drawings, perfect for framing (5" x 7"), or for crafting, scrapbooking, and making greeting cards!

Also great for working out your color schemes for the larger drawings.

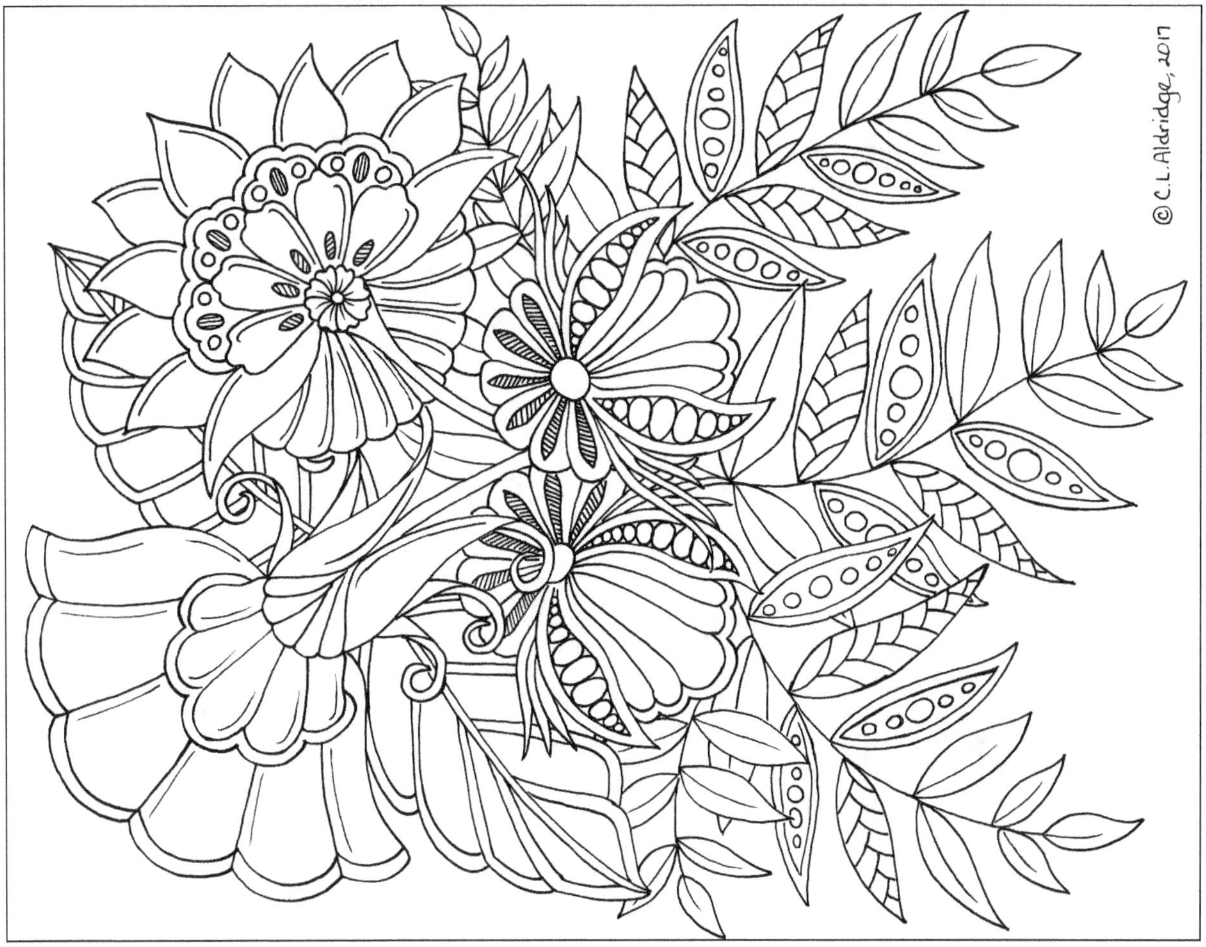

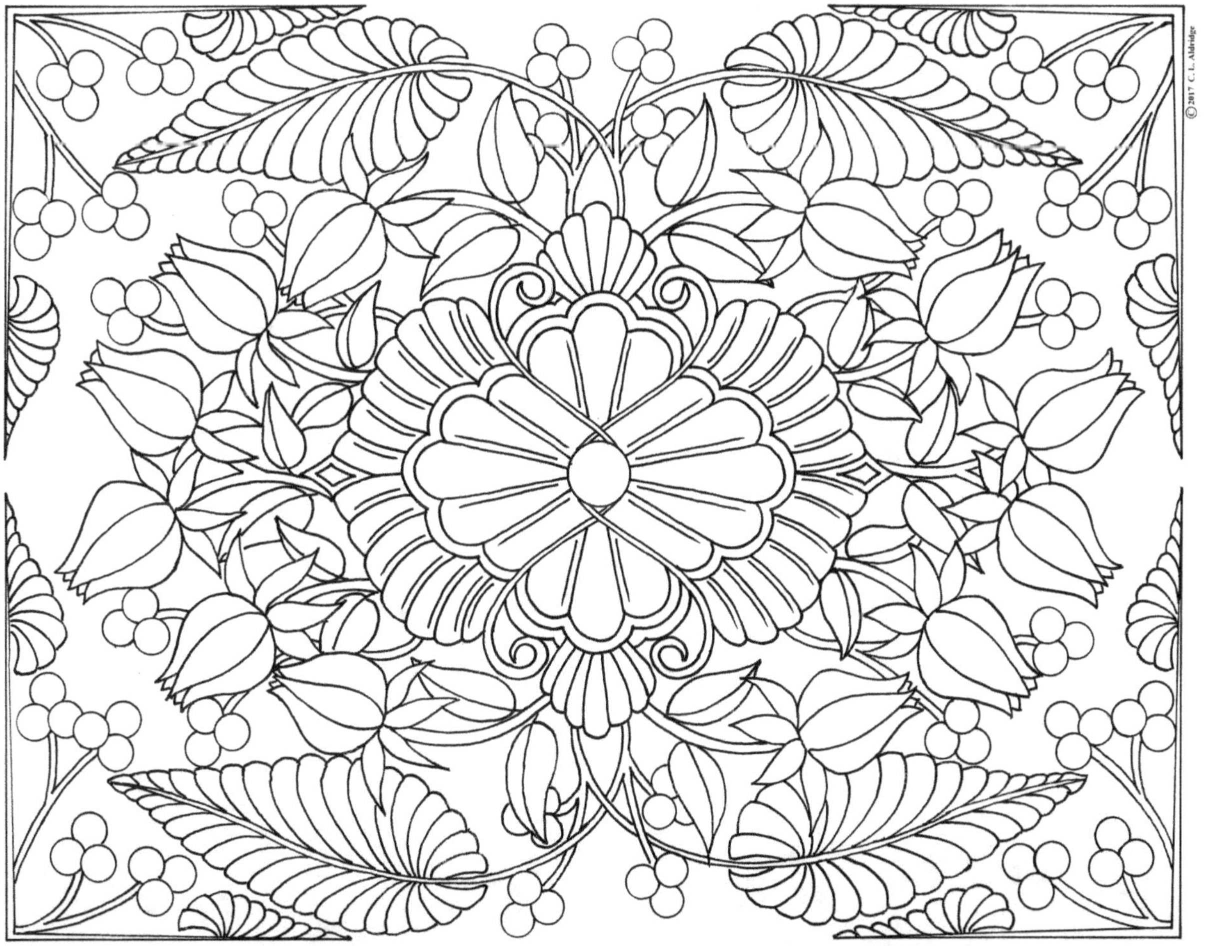

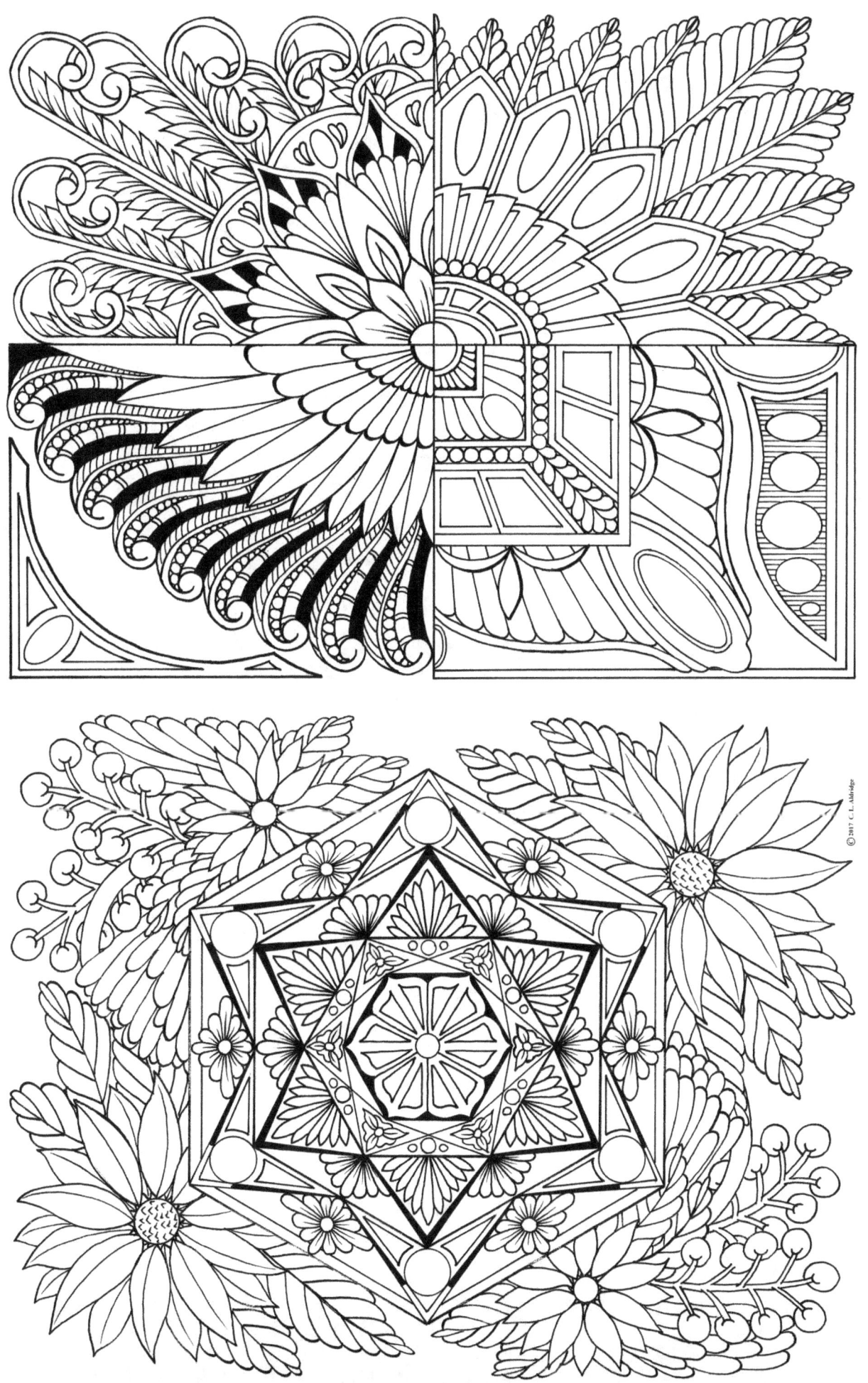

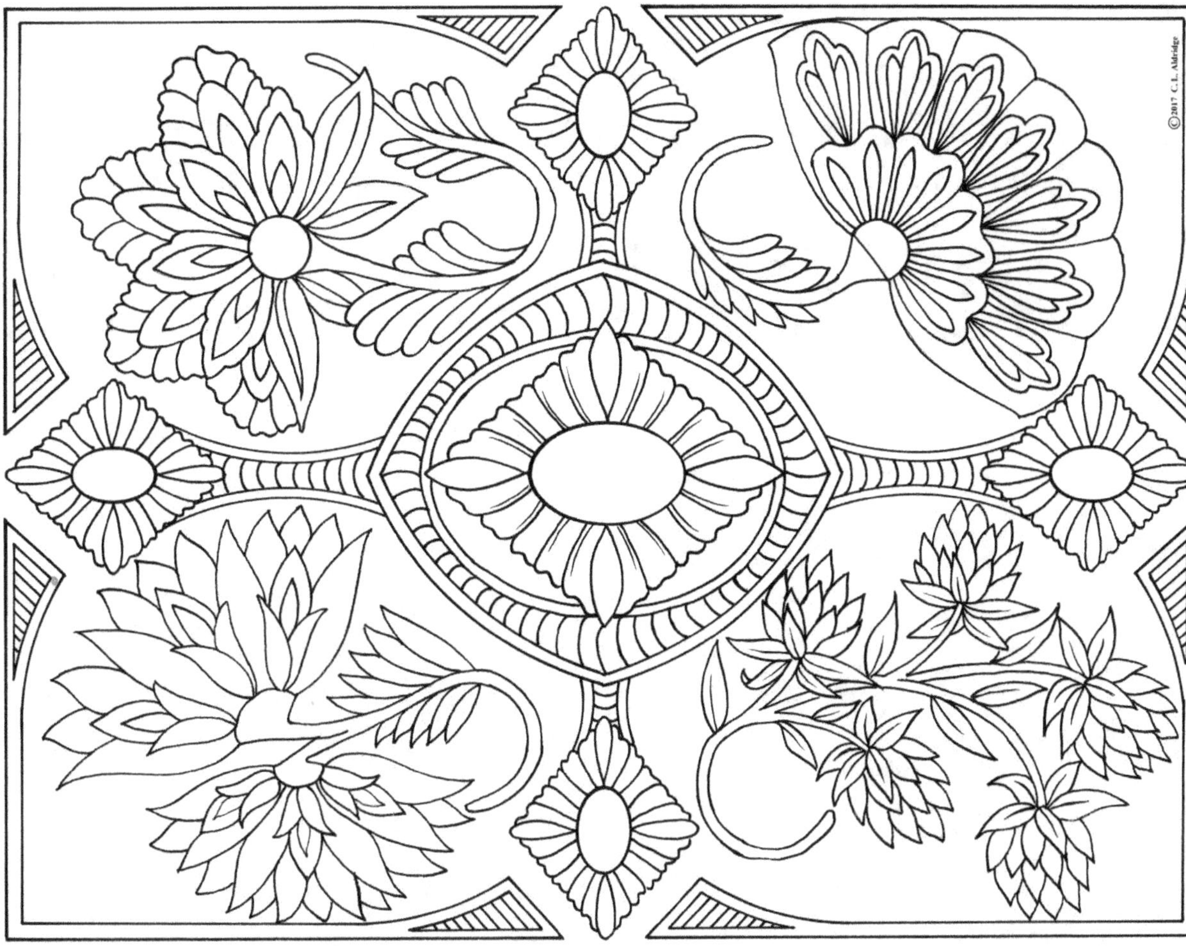

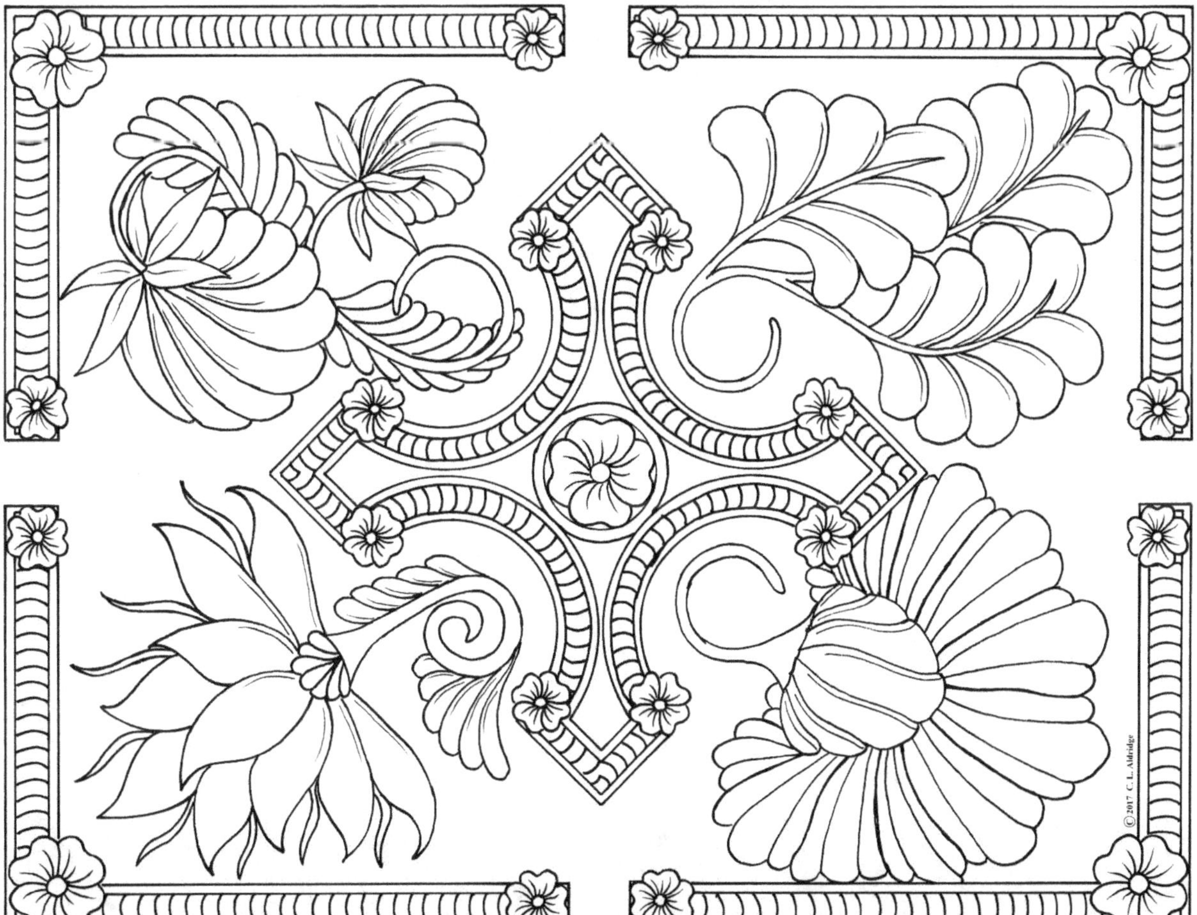

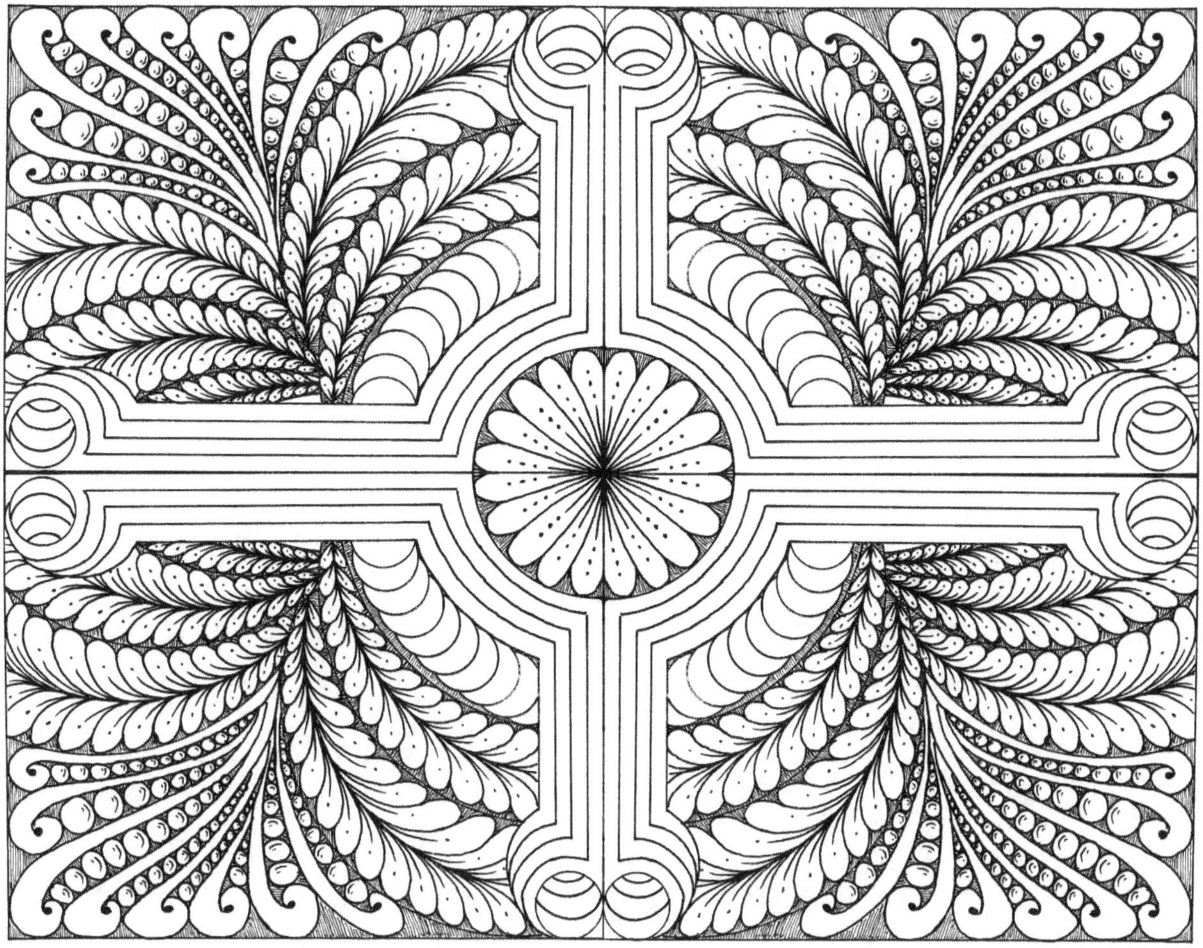

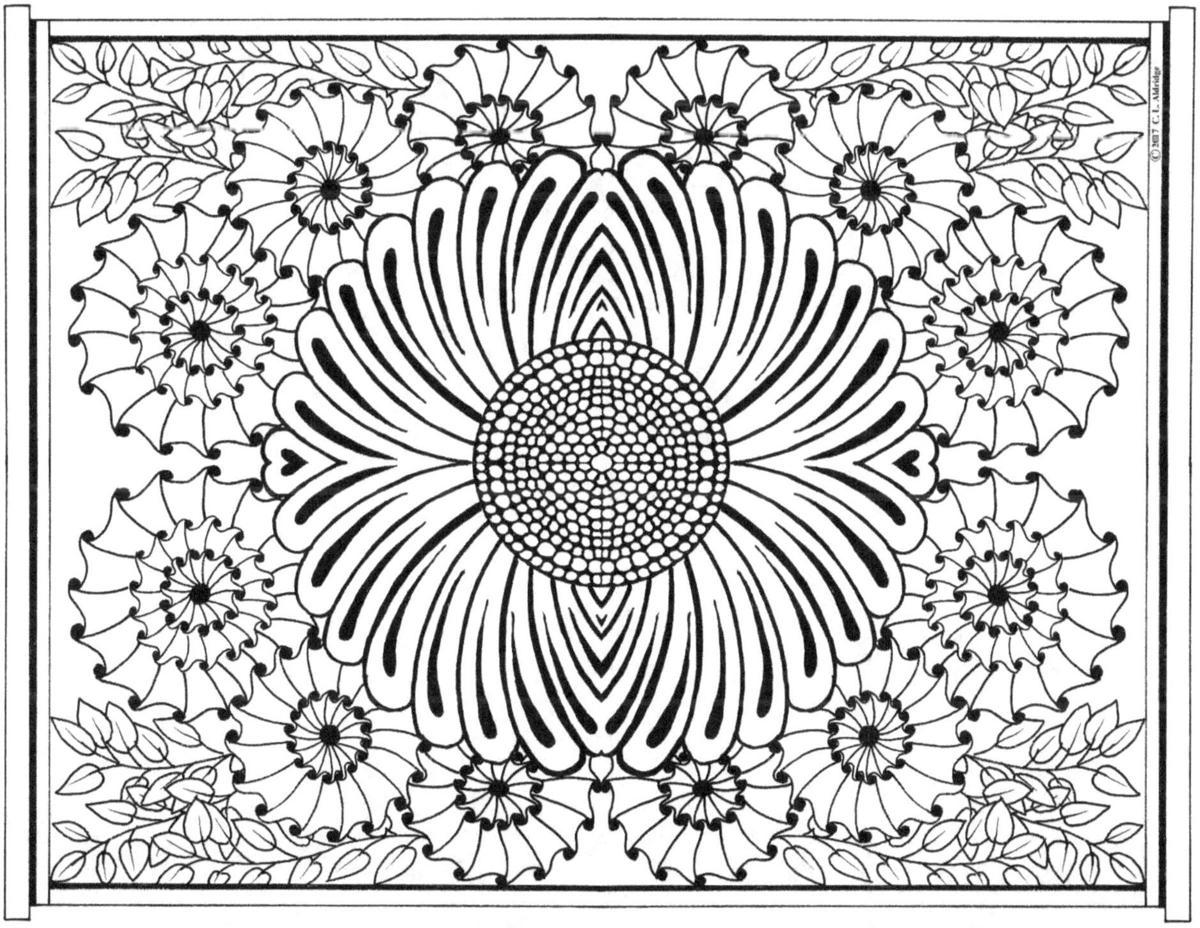

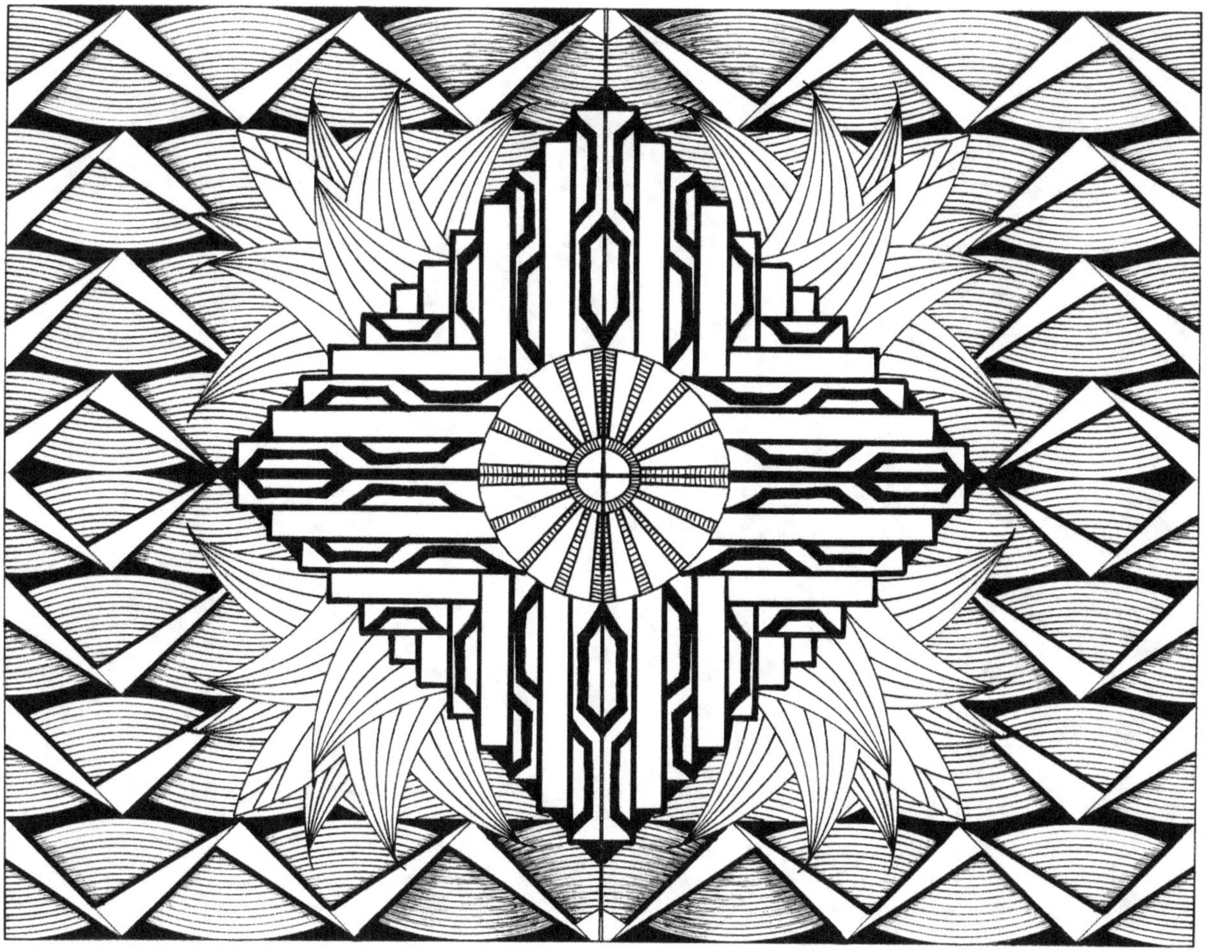

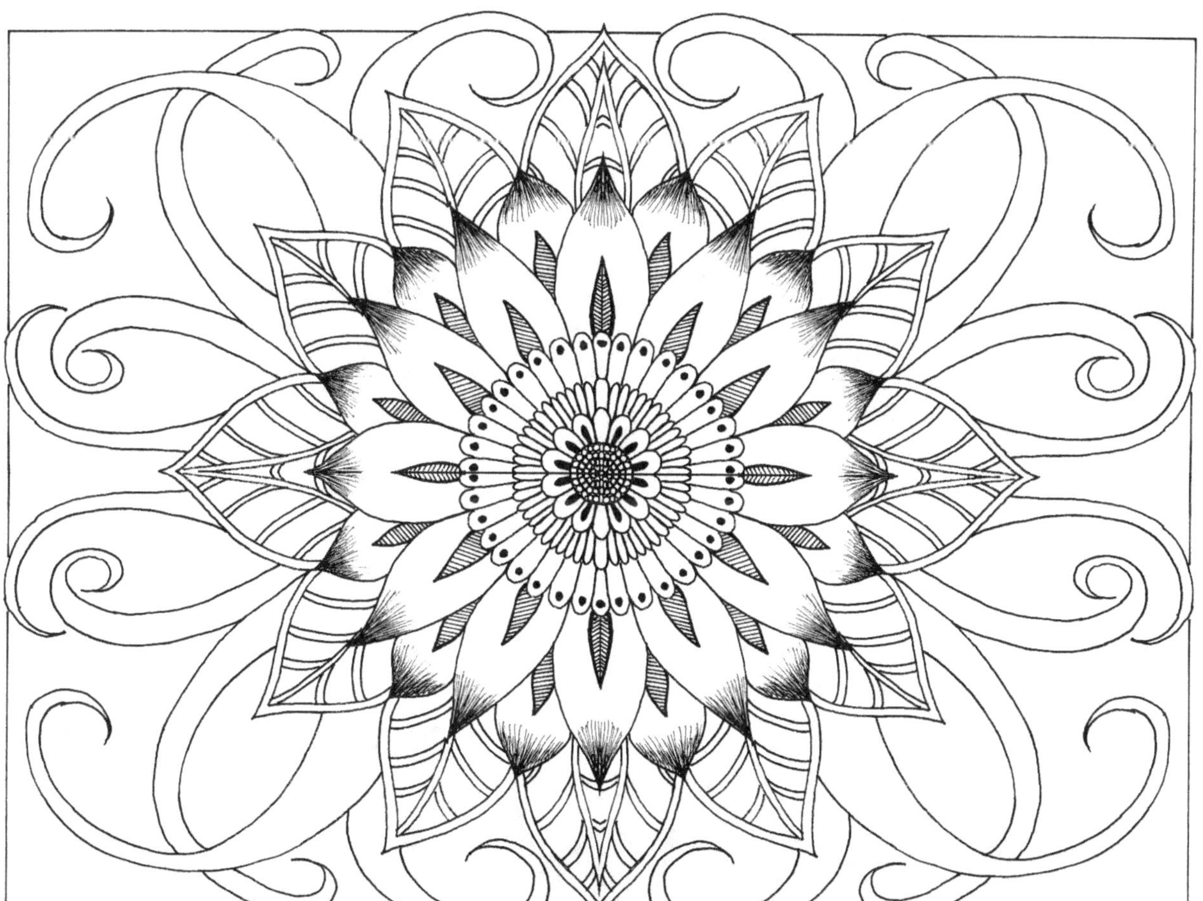

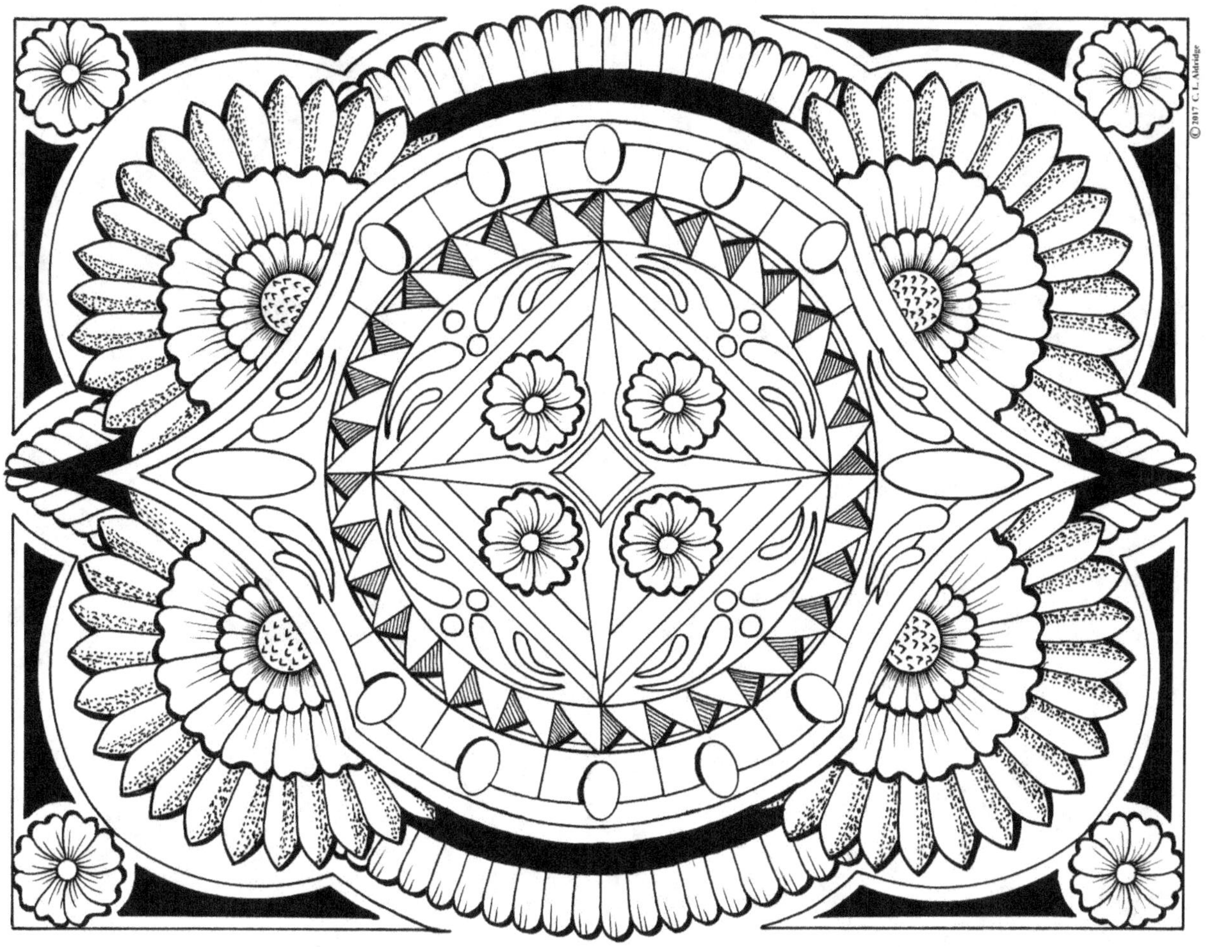

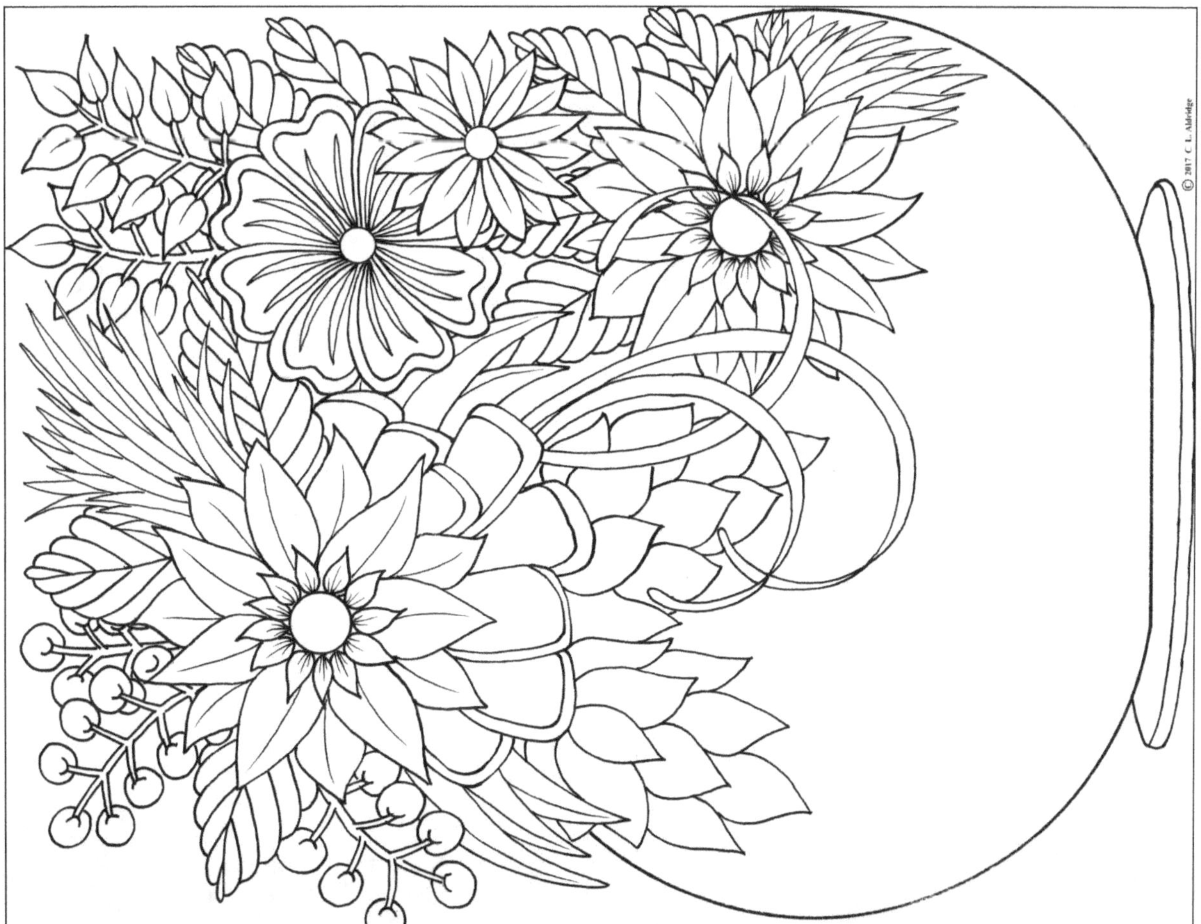

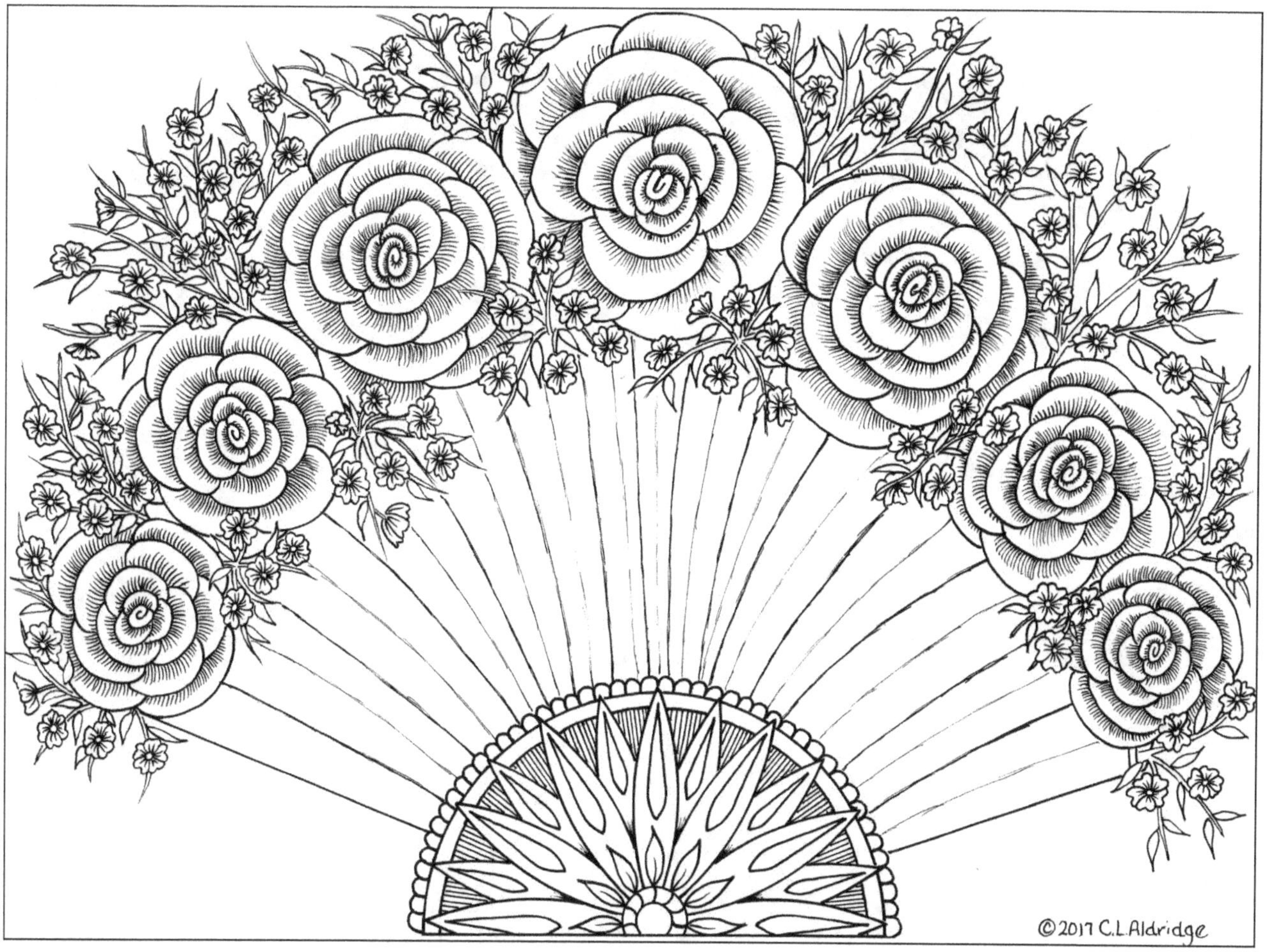

©2017 C.L. Aldridge

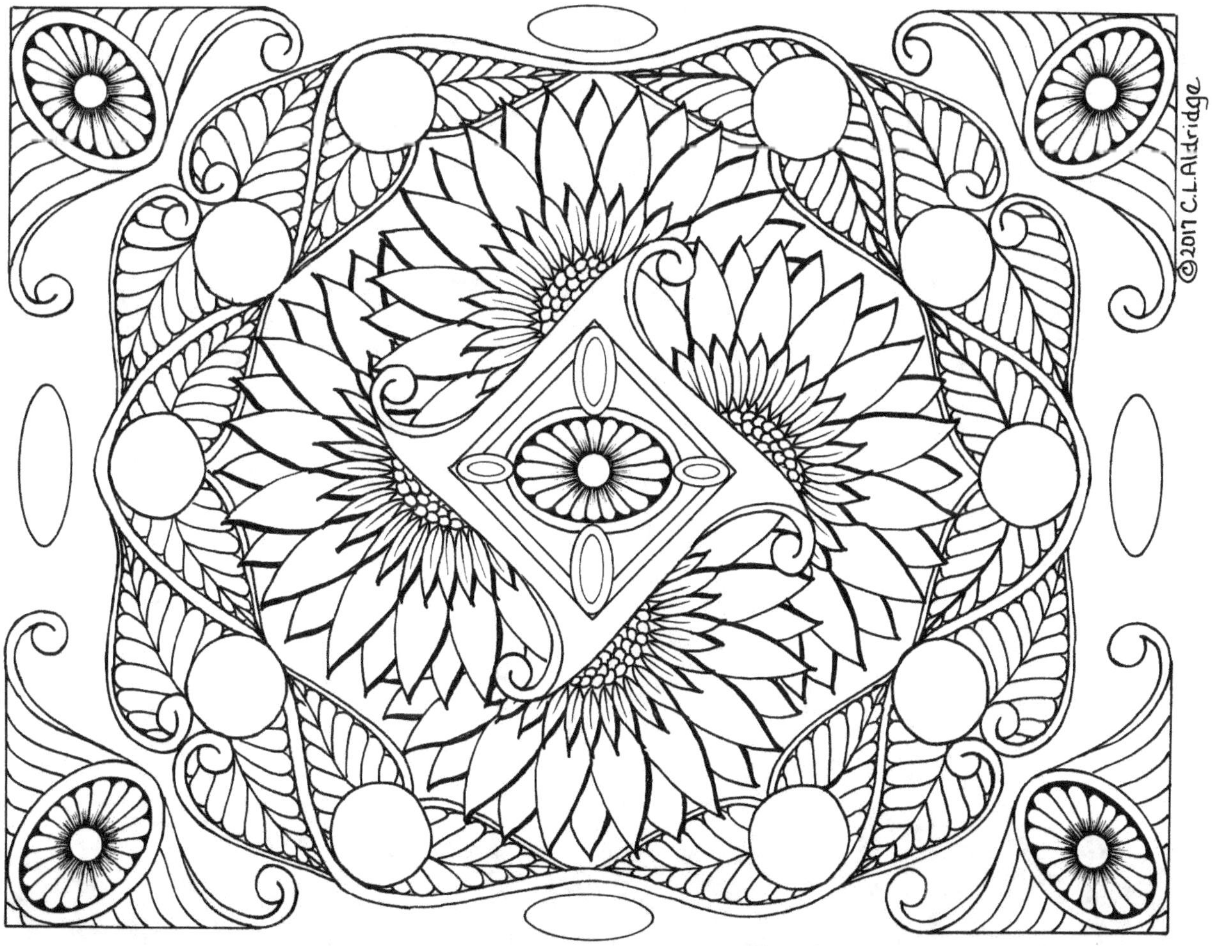

©2017 C.L. Aldridge

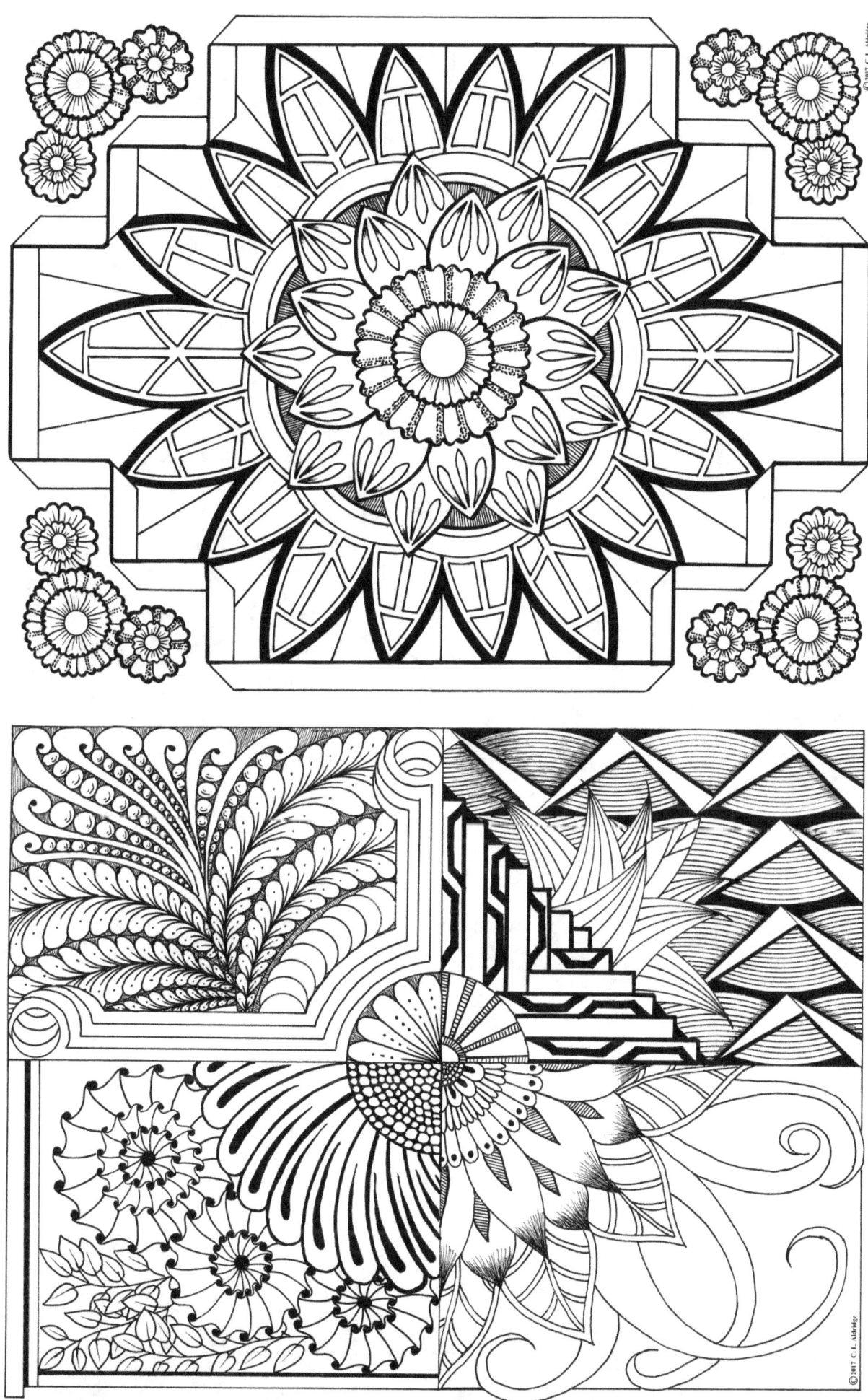

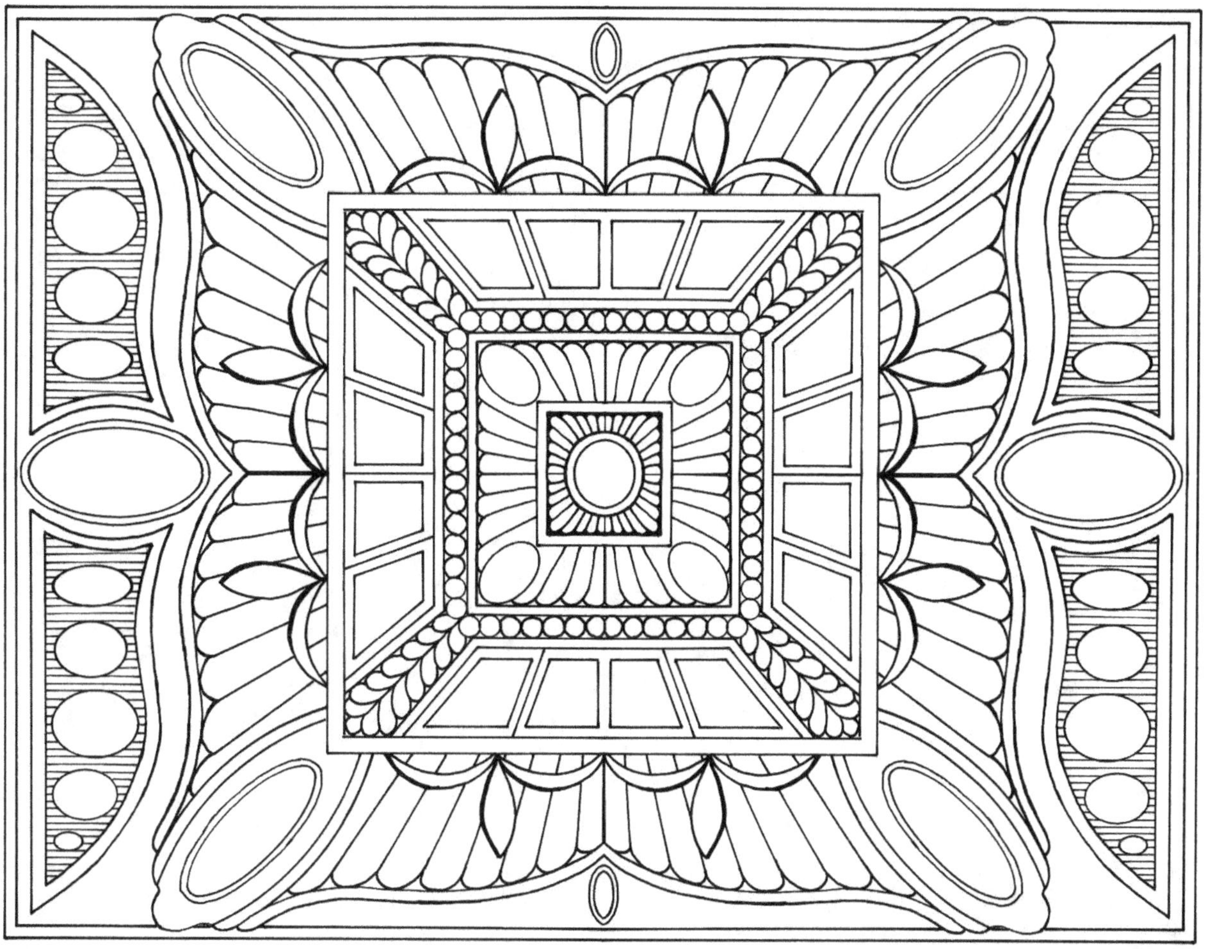

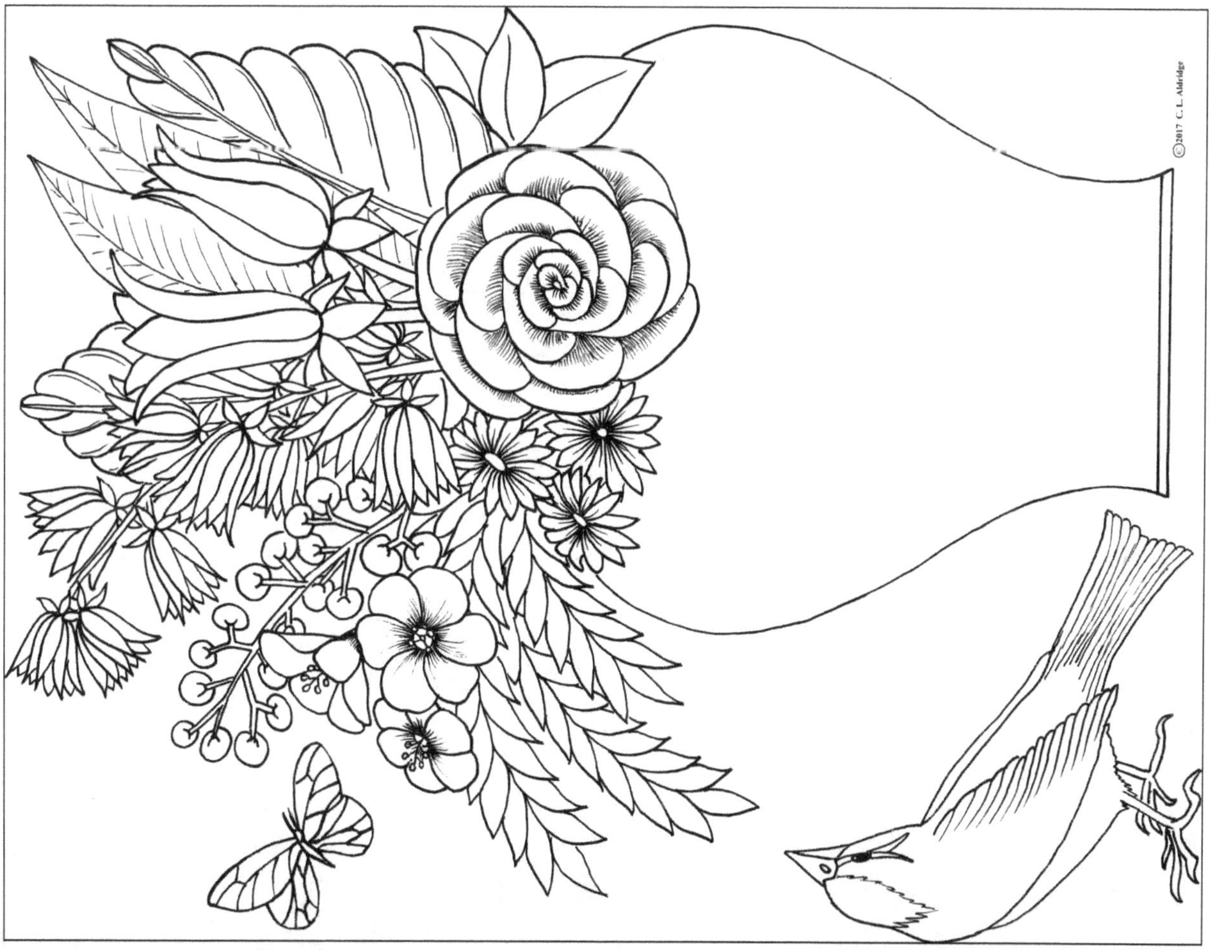

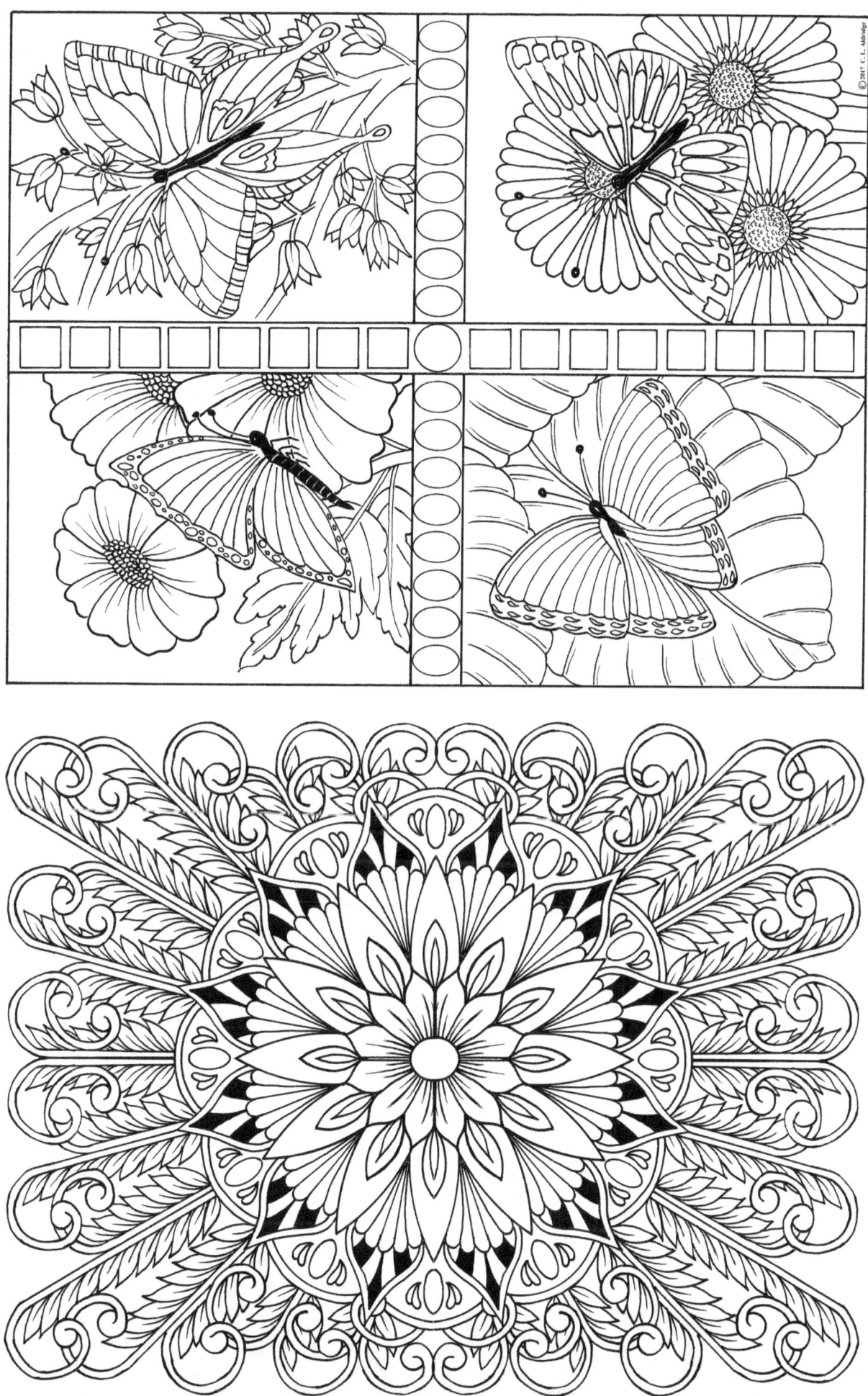

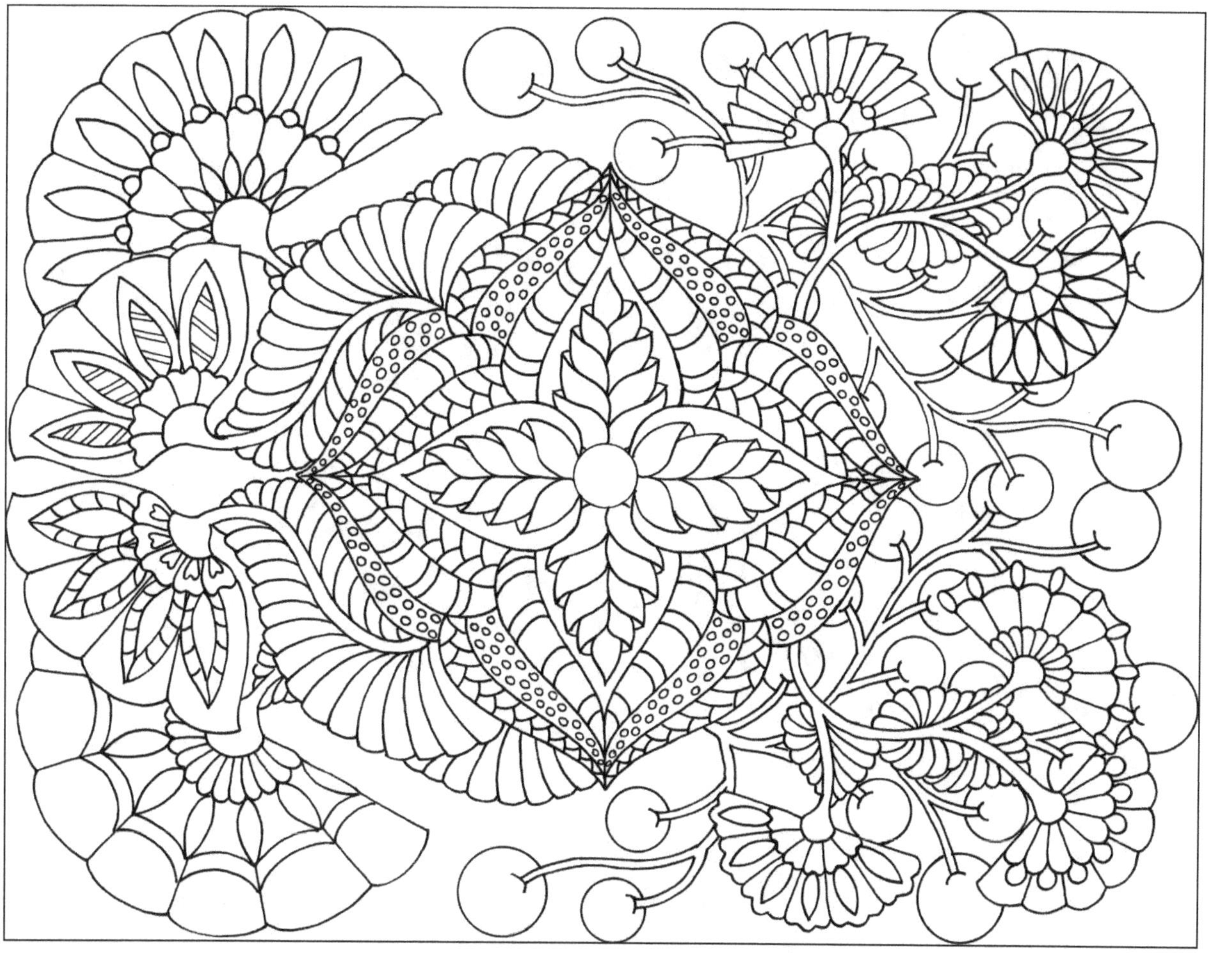

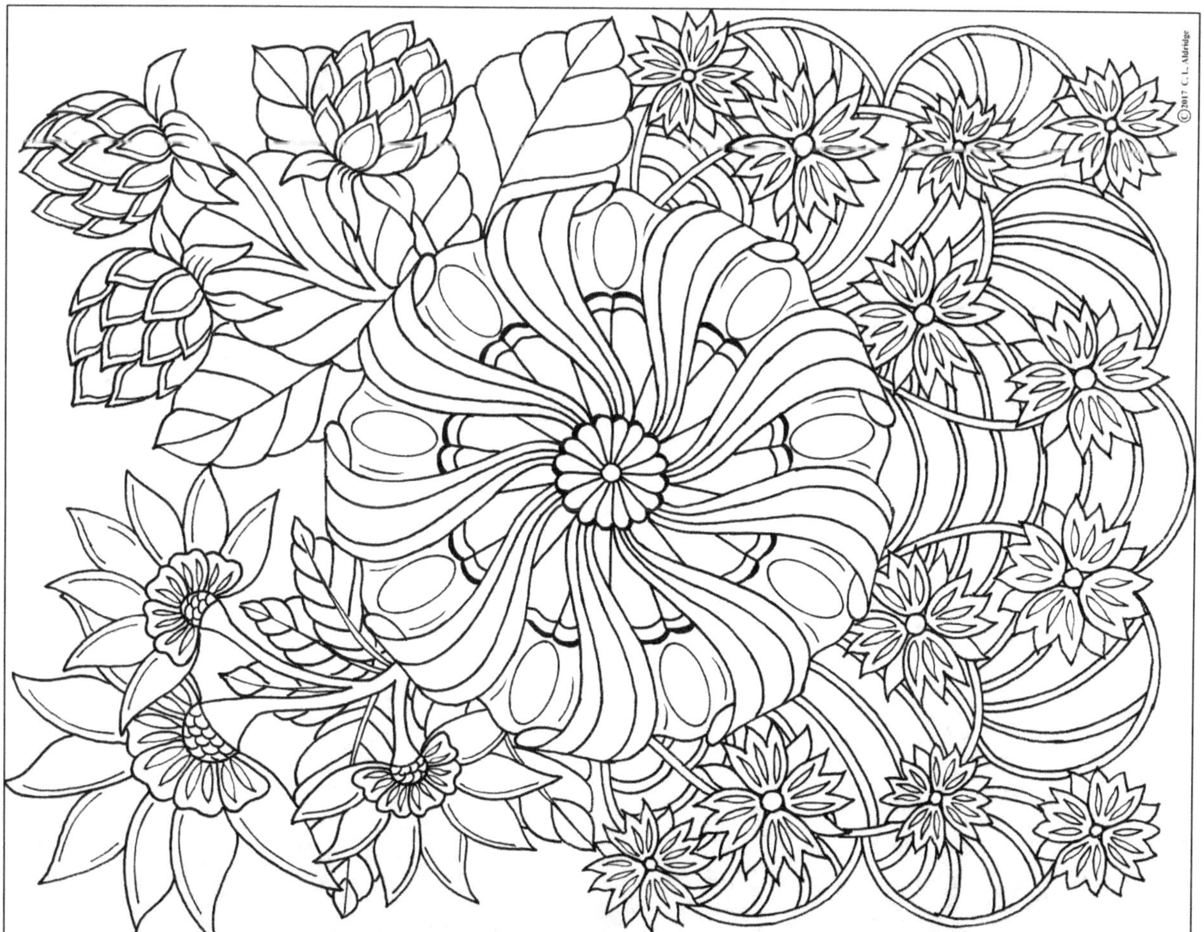

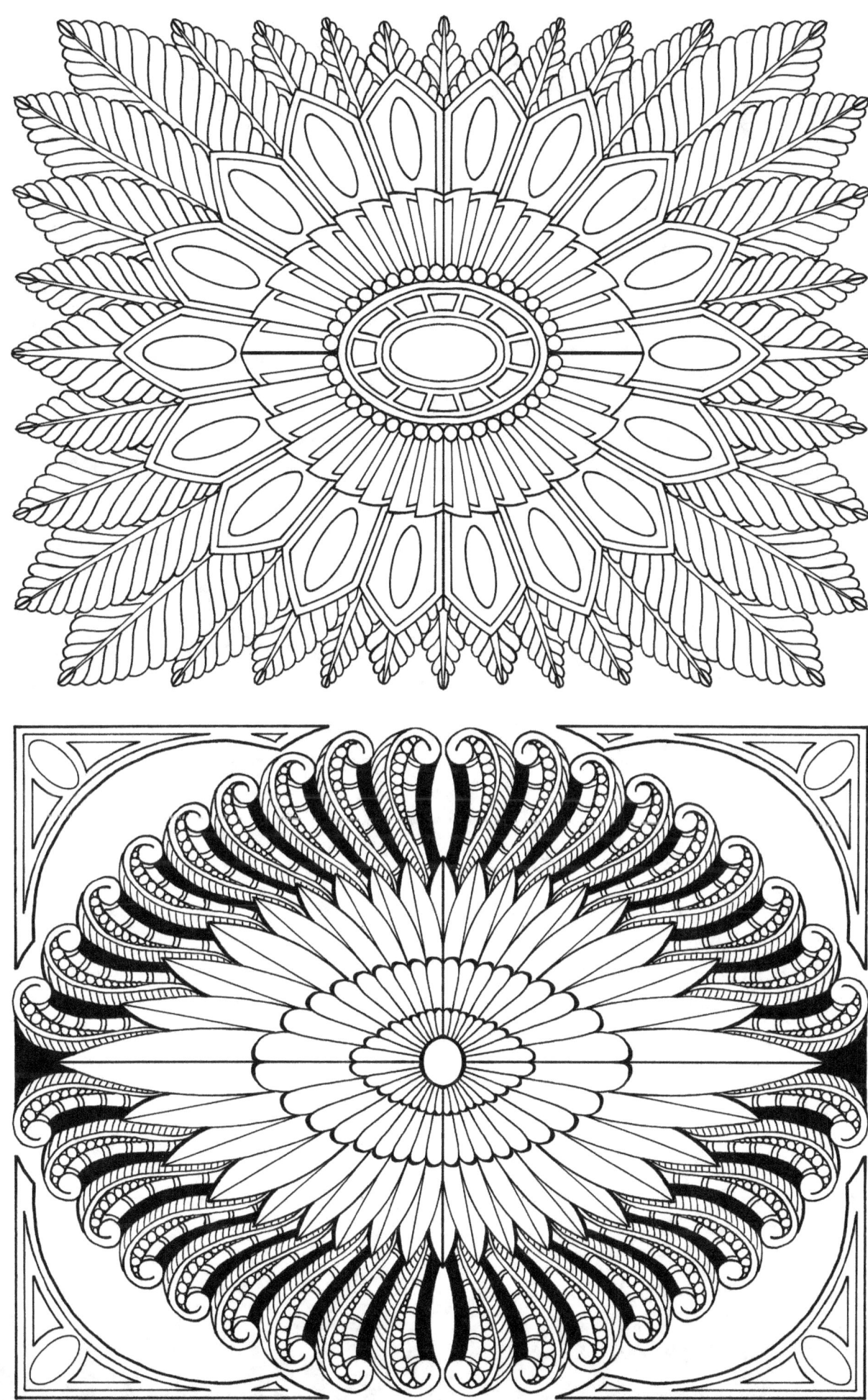

# BONUS PAGES

In order of placement, a SAMPLE PAGE from:

"Flowers and Dreams"
"The Adult Coloring Book of Flower Inspirations"
"Flowers and Flyers"
"Flowers and Whimsy"
"Flowers of Fantasy" (Vol 1)
Plus a previous unpublished drawing titled "Beach Fantasy"

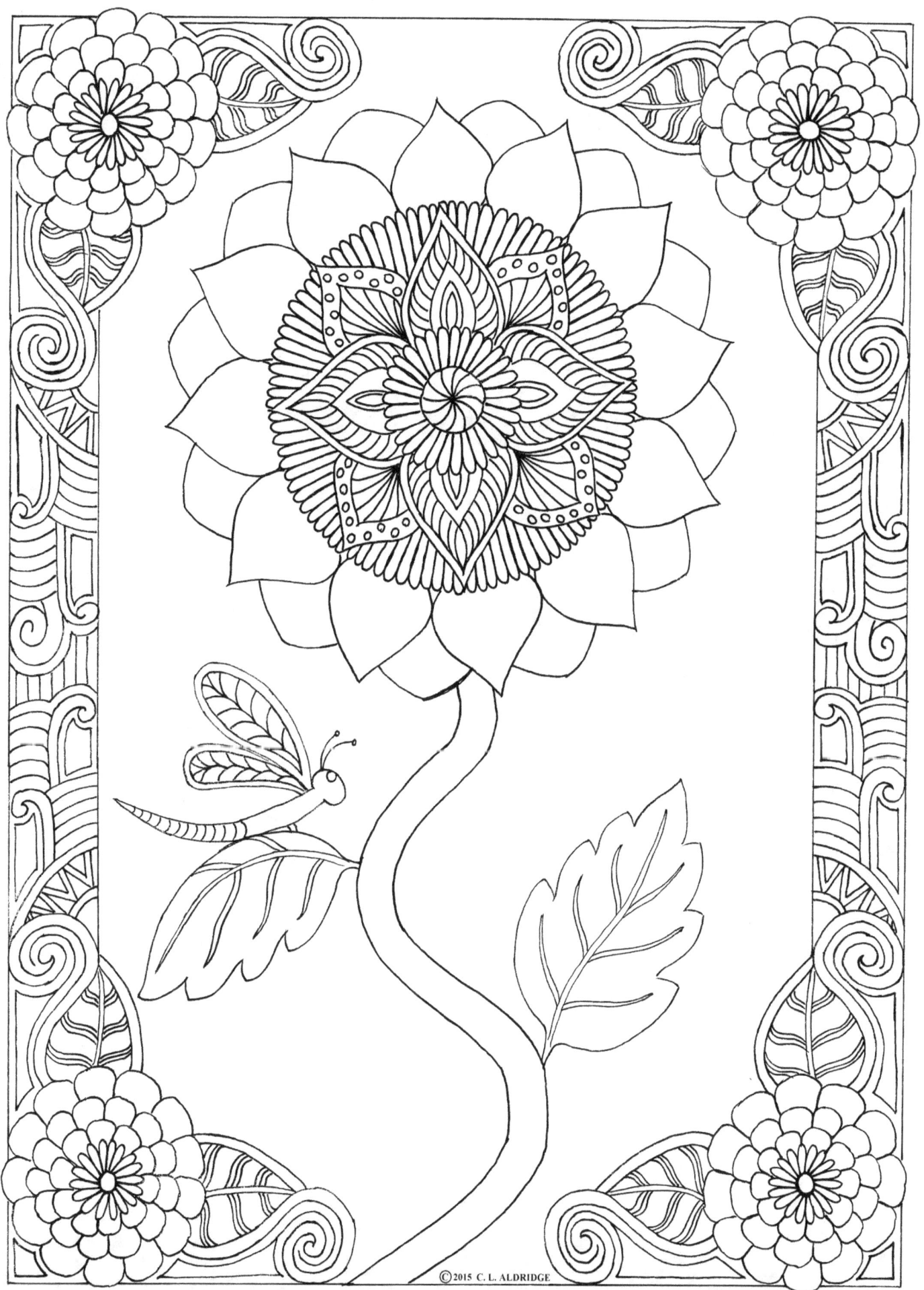

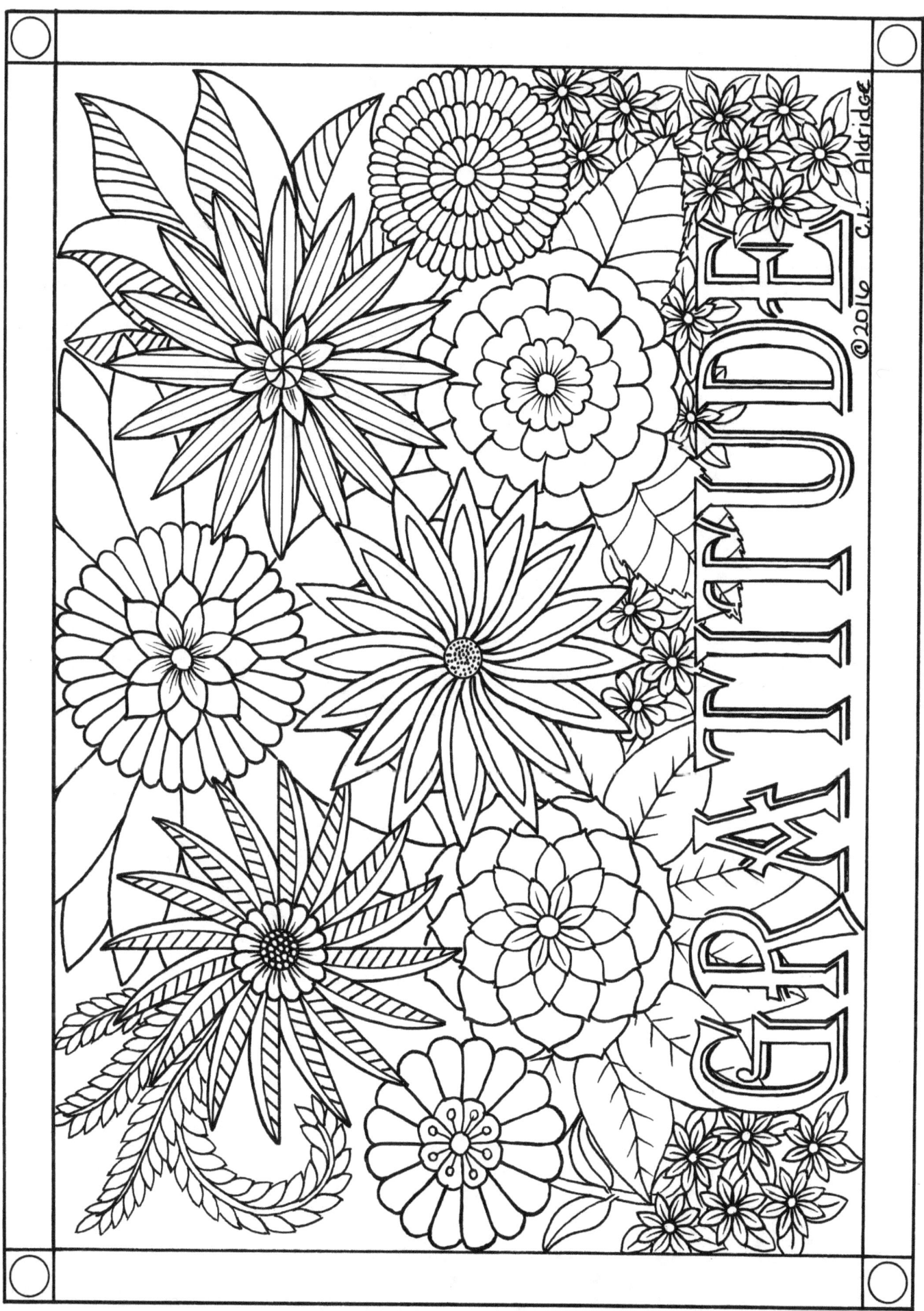

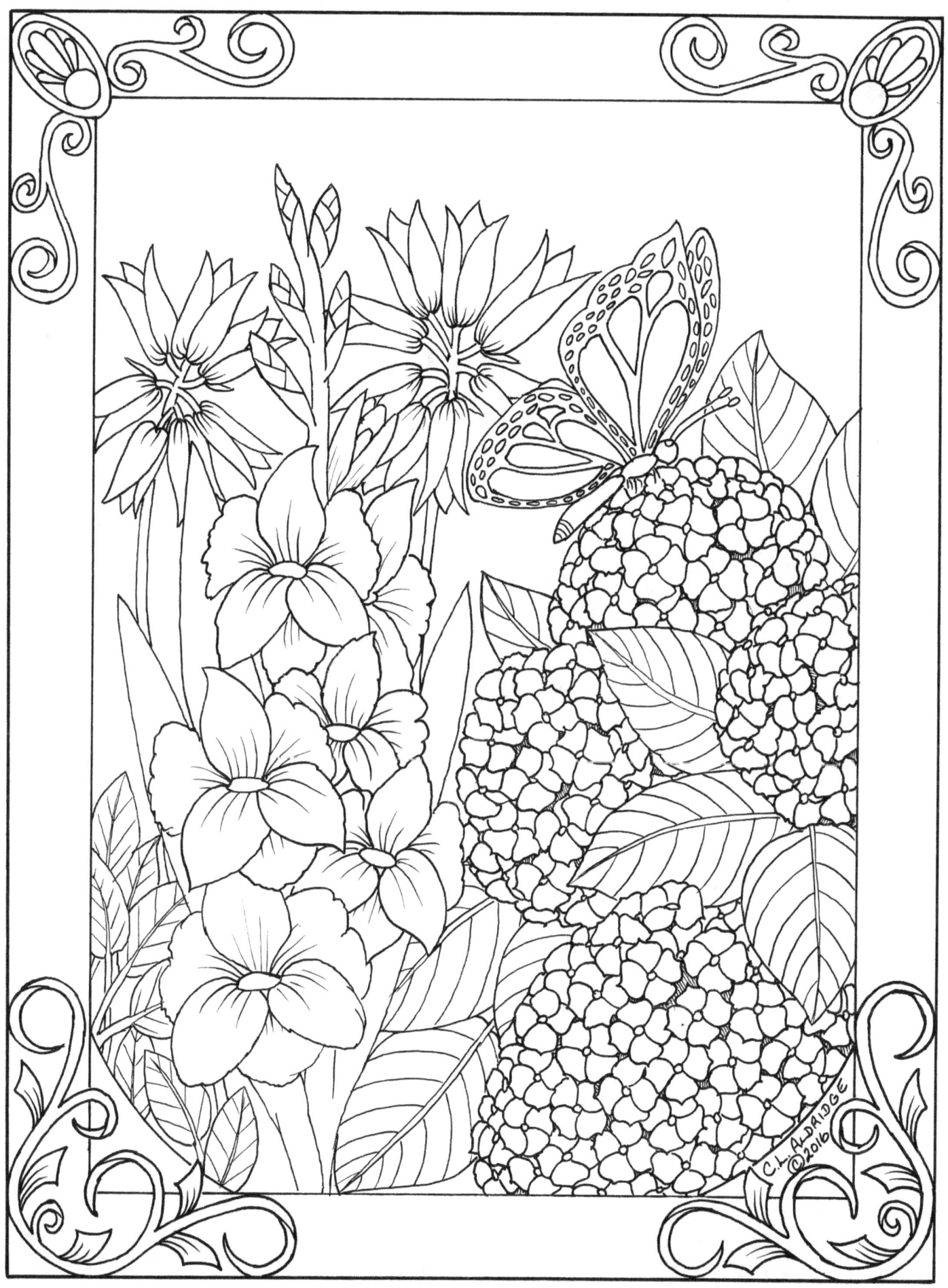

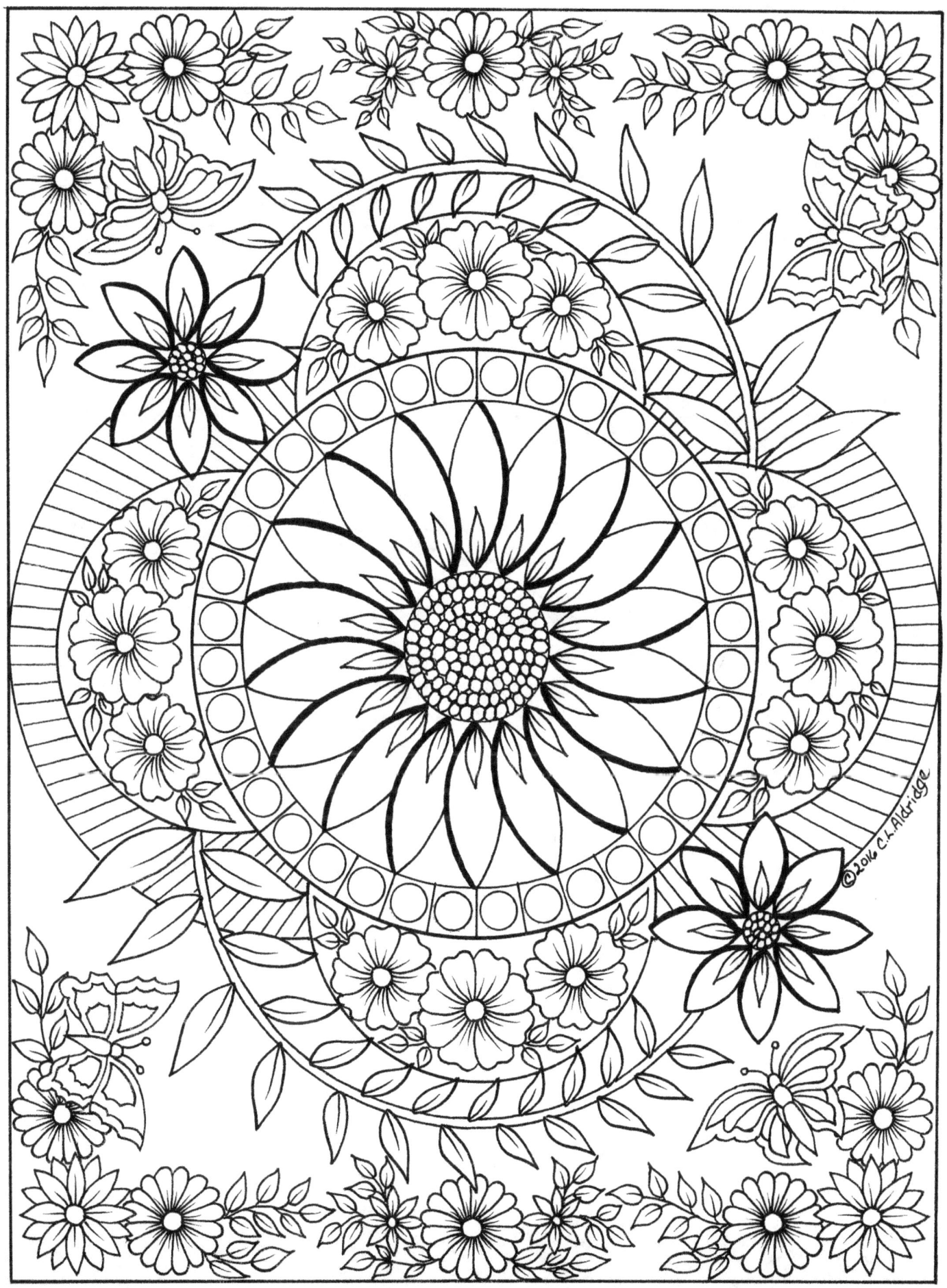

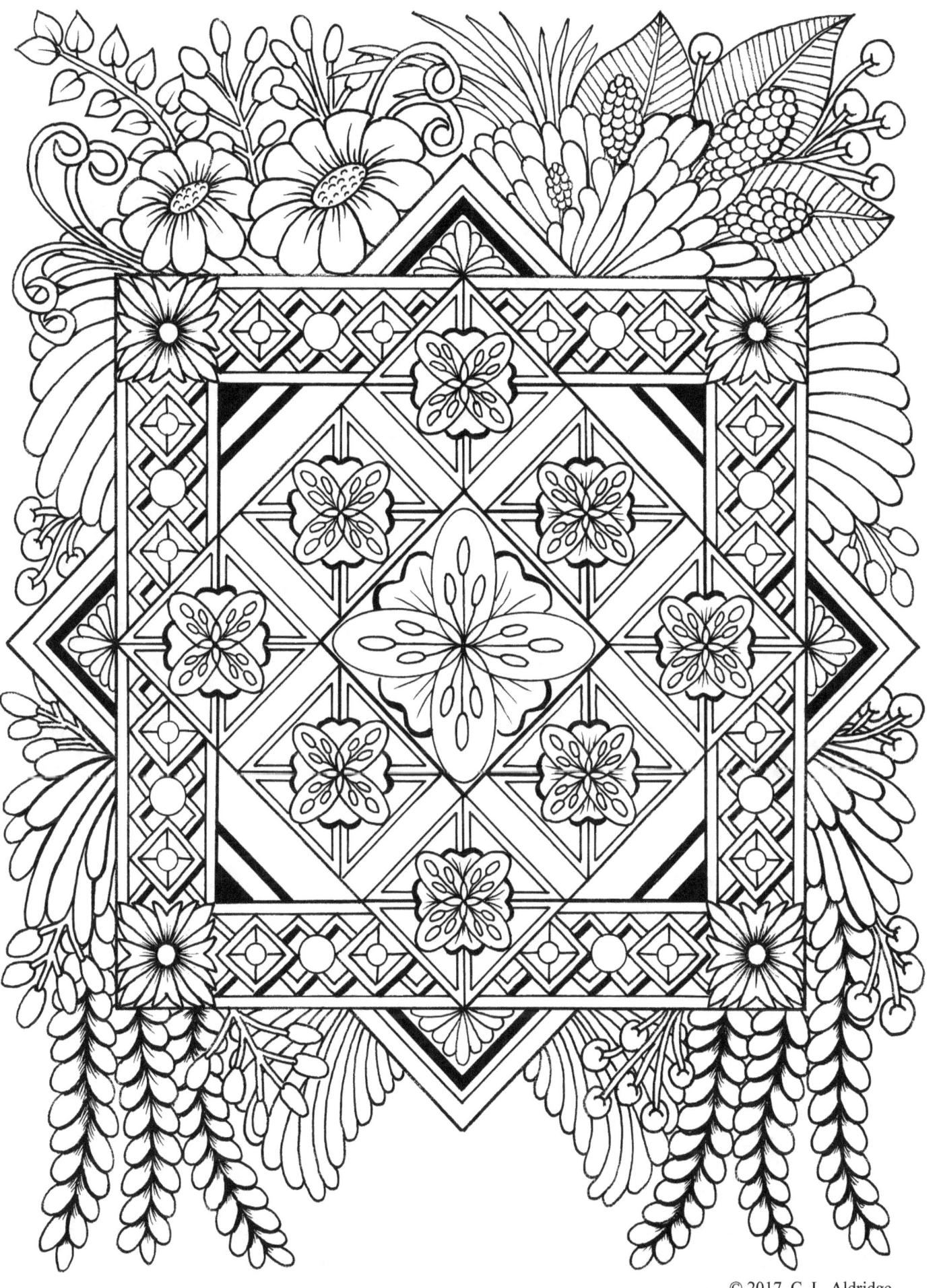

© 2017 C. L. Aldridge

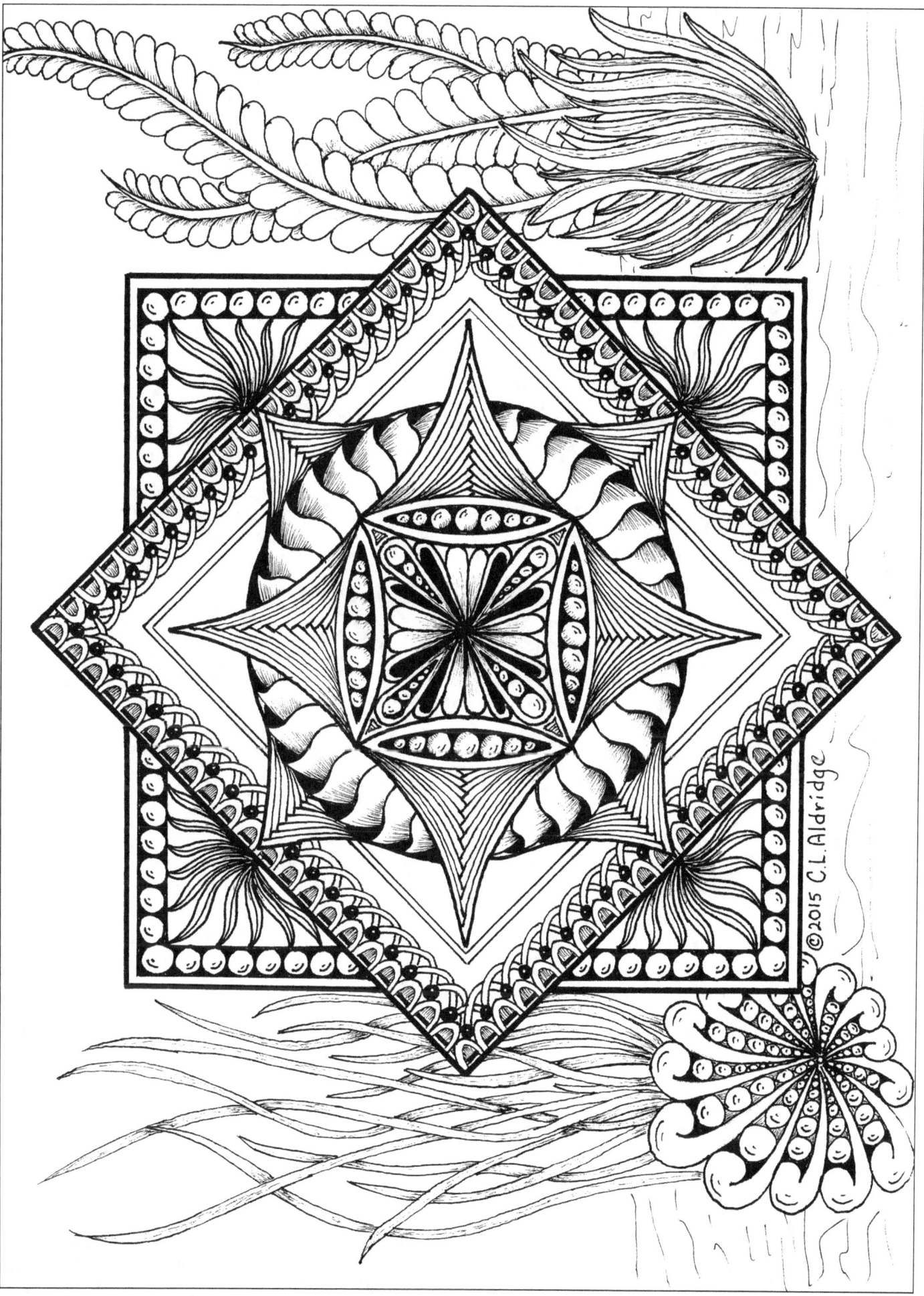

This page has intentionally been left blank for use as either a blotting page or color testing page.

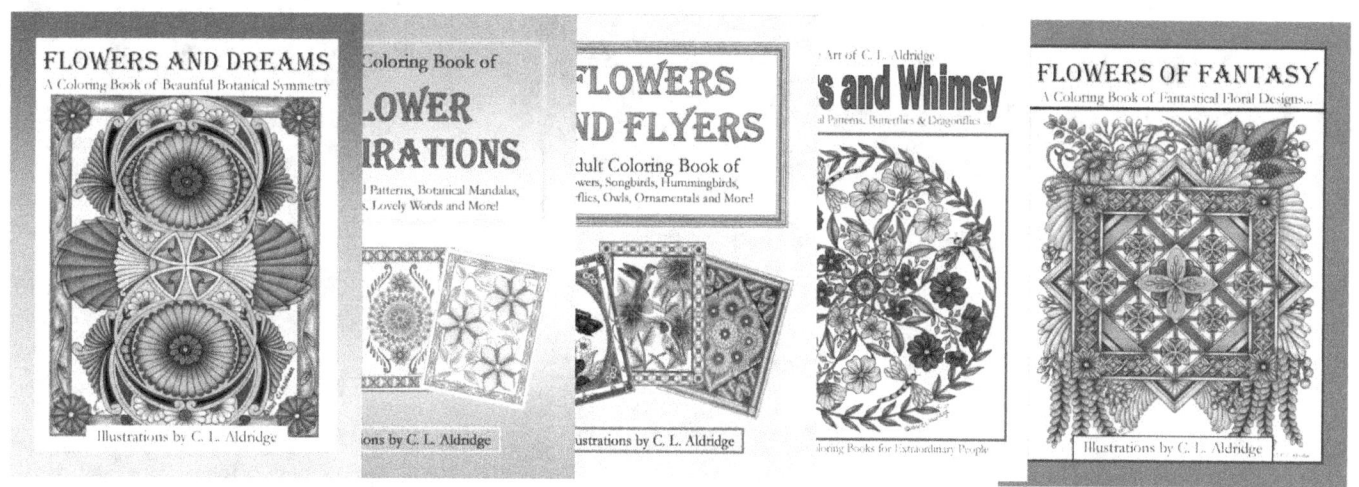

## Extraordinary Coloring Books for Extraordinary People

**Available in Print at Amazon.com Worldwide**
Or as a PDF at CLAldridgeArt on Etsy
NOW LOWEST PRICE EVER!!!

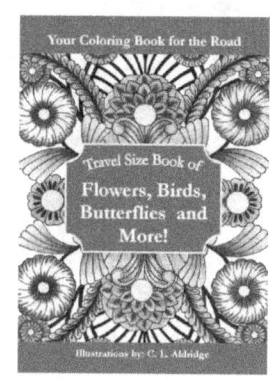

PLEASE COME JOIN US AT

## C. L. Aldridge's, Coloring In Bloom—Coloring Club

On FACEBOOK. Post your beautiful colorings and be inspired by the coloring of other fans of C. L. Aldridge Art, we'll leave a light on for you!

If you like these books, please consider leaving your review on Amazon.com